This book is dedicated to my wife Zora,
who shares all the facets of my life and inspires all that I do.

CONTENTS

Don't miss this book's companion website!

Turn the page for details.

**THE TECH SET® Volumes 11–20 is more than just the book
you're holding!**

These 10 titles, along with the 10 titles that preceded them, in THE TECH SET® series feature three components:

1. This book
2. Companion web content that provides more details on the topic and keeps you current
3. Author podcasts that will extend your knowledge and give you insight into the author's experience

The companion webpages and podcasts can be found at:

www.alatechsource.org/techset/

On the website, you'll go far beyond the printed pages you're holding and:

- ▶ Access author updates that are packed with new advice and recommended resources
- ▶ Use the website comments section to interact, ask questions, and share advice with the authors and your LIS peers
- ▶ Hear these pros in screencasts, podcasts, and other videos providing great instruction on getting the most out of the latest library technologies

For more information on THE TECH SET® series and the individual titles, visit **www.neal-schuman.com/techset-11-to-20**.

FOREWORD

Cloud computing offers organizations new cost-effective ways to use web services for their computing needs, including software applications, data storage, cloud development platforms, and processing power. This top-notch primer by cloud technology expert Marshall Breeding provides a comprehensive view of the cloud computing landscape, the types of solutions available, their benefits and limitations, and how to use them in your library. Learn how to leverage the cloud for e-mail and document sharing, storing media collections, hosting your library website, OPAC, or digital repository, and even powering a web-driven database in this one-stop passport to cloud computing. *Cloud Computing for Libraries* reveals how to harness the power of the cloud through well-known services such as Amazon Web Services and DuraCloud and even how to use Google App Engine to create your own cloud applications.

The ten new TECH SET volumes are designed to be even more cutting-edge than the original ten. After the first ten were published and we received such positive feedback from librarians who were using the books to implement technology in their libraries as well as train their staff, it seemed that there would be a need for another TECH SET. And I wanted this next set of books to be even more forward-looking and tackle today's hottest technologies, trends, and practices to help libraries stay on the forefront of technology innovation. Librarians have ceased sitting on the sidelines and have become technology leaders in their own right. This series was created to offer guidance and inspiration to all those aspiring to be library technology leaders themselves.

I originally envisioned a series of books that would offer accessible, practical information that would teach librarians not only how to use new technologies as individuals but also how to plan and implement particular types of library services using them. And when THE TECH SET won the ALA's Greenwood Publishing Group Award for the Best Book in Library Literature, it seemed that we had achieved our goal of becoming the go-to resource for libraries wanting hands-on technology primers. For these new ten books, I thought it was important to incorporate reader feedback by adding two new chapters that would better facilitate learning how to put these new technologies into practice in libraries. The new chapter called "Social Mechanics" discusses strategies for gaining buy-in and support from organizational stakeholders, and the additional "Developing Trends" chapter looks ahead to future directions of these technologies. These new chapters round out the books that discuss the entire life cycle of these tech initiatives, including everything from what it takes to plan, strategize, implement, market, and measure the success of these projects.

While each book covers the A–Zs of each technology being discussed, the hands-on "Implementation" chapters, chock-full of detailed project instructions, account for the largest portions of the books. These chapters start off with a basic "recipe" for how to effectively use the technology in a library and then build on that foundation to offer more and more advanced project ideas. Because these books are designed to appeal to readers of all levels of expertise, both the novice and advanced technologist will find something useful in these chapters, as the proposed projects and initiatives run the gamut from the basic how to create a Foursquare campaign for your library to how to build an iPhone application. Similarly, the new Drupal webmaster will benefit from the instructions for how to configure a basic library website, while the advanced web services librarian may be interested in the instructions for powering a dynamic library website in the cloud using Amazon's EC2 service.

I have been watching and learning from Marshall Breeding's presentations and publications for many years now. And when I realized that the series should include a book on cloud computing, I knew that he needed to write it. Marshall's extensive knowledge and experience really shine through in this outstanding book, *Cloud Computing for Libraries*. If you want to learn all there is to know about the cloud and how to effectively leverage it in your library, this is the book for you.

Ellyssa Kroski
Manager of Information Systems
New York Law Institute
http://www.ellyssakroski.com/
http://oedb.org/blogs/ilibrarian/
ellyssakroski@yahoo.com

Ellyssa Kroski is the Manager of Information Systems at the New York Law Institute as well as a writer, educator, and international conference speaker. In 2011, she won the ALA's Greenwood Publishing Group Award for the Best Book in Library Literature for THE TECH SET, the ten-book technology series that she created and edited. She's also the author of *Web 2.0 for Librarians and Information Professionals*, a well-reviewed book on web technologies and libraries. She speaks at several conferences a year, mainly about new tech trends, digital strategy, and libraries. She is an adjunct faculty member at Pratt Institute and blogs at *iLibrarian*.

PREFACE

In a time when the term "cloud computing" seems tagged to almost any kind of technology product to make it sound new and trendy, *Cloud Computing for Libraries* distinguishes the substance from the hype to make you well-equipped to understand and evaluate its merits, risks, and value to your organization.

Cloud computing represents one of the most important technology trends of our time. Every day we make use of computing and information resources through a web browser powered by some distant and diffuse infrastructure. This model has become routine for personal use—e-mail, word processing, social networking, photo sharing. In more recent months and years cloud computing has entered the library technology sphere. Cloud computing brings the opportunity for libraries to shift away from the need to own and operate their own servers to power their core automation applications and to instead shift to gaining similar functionality through web-based services. In order to develop technology strategies in this context, it's essential for libraries to have a solid understanding of this new technology landscape, to move beyond a vague awareness of cloud computing to a more nuanced, well-informed understanding of such concepts as software-as-a-service, infra-structure-as-a-service, and platform-as-a-service and the relative advantages, caveats, and risks.

▶ AUDIENCE AND ORGANIZATION

Cloud Computing for Libraries aims to equip libraries with the information and practical advice needed to evaluate the many opportunities to take advantages of cloud computing for the benefit of their organizations. It includes informa-tion on different levels; library administrators will gain the background needed to inform strategic planning relative to the broad changes adopting cloud computing effects in a library and its implications for budget and personnel; librarians throughout the organization will find ideas on how cloud computing applications can empower them to use technology without the constraints often present with locally supported infrastructure; systems librarians and other personnel who work more directly with technology will find in-depth information and examples of how they can roll up their sleeves and plunge directly into practical projects—often taking advantage of free levels of service offered by some of the top cloud services providers. It offers examples that can be followed by smaller libraries self-sufficient in their computing needs as well as those libraries that operate within large organizations with enterprise-oriented technology infrastructure. Public, academic, school, and special libraries all face similar issues as cloud computing grows to become the dominant way through which new technology services are delivered.

In the pages that follow, Chapter 1 sets the stage, providing a general overview of the concepts surrounding cloud computing. Chapter 2 begins to dig into the details by stepping through the various models of computing from those based on local infrastructure through increasing levels of abstraction through those more truly in the mold of cloud computing. Chapter 3 covers planning issues and the benefits and caveats that need to be part of any discussion or strategic decision regarding the computing infrastructure, such as whether to remain with local equipment or shift to a service-based alternative. This chapter also takes a look at the way that library automation products have embraced cloud computing. Given the major investments made in core library automation platforms, Chapter 4 takes a close look at how these products and services are increasingly offered through some form of cloud computing.

Libraries ready to begin experimenting with cloud computing, implement a pilot project, or engage in a full-blown implementation will see examples in Chapter 5, including the general procedures to follow. These examples serve both as some specific ways to get started with some of the major cloud services providers, such as those offered through Amazon Web Services and Google Apps, and inspiration to spark ideas for other ways to exploit these technologies.

Once a library chooses and implements a new service based on cloud computing, it's time to market it. Chapter 6 explores ideas on how to cultivate buy-in from library personnel and to boost the use of the service through direct promotional activities, improved usability, and search engine optimization. Chapter 7 offers best practices and some tips on how libraries can approach this new style of computing with the best advantage and least risk, and Chapter 8 turns to some of the ways that libraries can measure the use of these services and assess their impact. Finally, Chapter 9 examines some of the current and future trends to anticipate regarding how cloud computing will impact libraries and other organizations.

After reading *Cloud Computing for Libraries*, staff from all parts of the library will gain the conceptual and practical information they need to explore and exploit cloud computing to facilitate their own work and to benefit the library as a whole. This new approach to technology has the potential to help libraries offer new and innovative services and to direct their technology resources with more focused impact.

▶1

INTRODUCTION

▶ **A "Cloudy" View of the Future**

▶ **Evolving toward Cloud Computing Today**

▶ **The Many Forms of Cloud Computing**

▶ **Contrasting Example: Local Computing**

▶ **A Utility Model of Computing**

▶ **Benefits**

Technology can be complex, expensive, and difficult to manage. Many libraries find themselves severely constrained because they don't have adequate specialized personnel and sufficient funding to use technology to its full potential. Cloud computing can help turn the tables, lowering the thresholds of expense and expertise. While this model may not be a good fit for all libraries, or for all the different ways that libraries rely on technology, it's an option worth investigating and adopting when appropriate and beneficial. You can begin by experimenting with free or low-cost projects, moving along with more strategic components of technology infrastructure over time. This book aims to give you a clear understanding of this new approach to technology and how it can help a library by making technology more manageable and more cost-effective.

What Is Cloud Computing?

"Cloud computing" is not a precise term, with various definitions given; some examples:

According to *Wikipedia*: "Cloud computing is Internet-based computing, whereby shared resources, software, and information are provided to computers and other devices on demand, like the electricity grid." (http://en.wikipedia.org/wiki/Cloud_computing)

VMware, a company involved in providing software and services, offers a more business-oriented definition: "Cloud computing is a new approach that reduces IT complexity by leveraging the efficient pooling of on-demand, self-managed virtual infrastructure, consumed as a service." (http://www.vmware.com/ap/cloud-computing.html)

Cloud computing takes its name from the way that it's fuzzy, distant, diffuse, and immense. This approach to technology relies on massive aggregations of hardware that form an amorphous mass that as a whole delivers some kind of computing activity. You can't see or touch the cloud—its actual pieces and parts are scattered in data centers, whose exact physical locations you may or may not know.

The term "cloud computing" is used quite freely, tagged to almost any type of virtualized computing environment or any arrangement where the library relies on a remote hosting environment for a major automation component. It's as much a marketing term as a technical one. Some of its characteristics include:

► An abstract technology platform that involves generalized access to remote computing resources rather than locally owned and managed discrete servers
► A utility model of computing involving fees charged for levels of use rather than capital investments in hardware or permanent software licenses
► Computing that's provisioned on demand, with resources allocated as needed
► Elastic quantity and power of the computing resources that increase at times of peak use and scale down when demand is lower
► Highly clustered and distributed computing infrastructure that spreads computing tasks across many devices to maximize performance with high fault tolerance for the failure of individual components

Cloud computing isn't an all-or-nothing proposition. A library can continue to manage some parts of its computing operation on locally managed servers as it makes selective use of cloud services. For those more open to experimentation, there are lots of opportunities to try out some cloud-based services or create prototypes to gain firsthand knowledge of its approach and how it might benefit the library. It's easy to start trying out services delivered in the cloud for one's personal computing needs. Introducing cloud computing into an organization such as a library requires a bit more thought and planning.

Today there's lots of hype surrounding cloud computing. Like any new technology, it has its enthusiasts and its detractors. There are lots of companies that offer their services through the cloud, and naturally they promote this approach and emphasize its benefits and downplay the risks and disadvantages. As libraries consider moving their essential services to the cloud, it's essential to separate hype from substance. This book will present both sides of the story, including the potential benefits and any caveats that might apply. Most of all, it will provide you with a clear understanding of the general concepts and with enough details of the various approaches and service offerings that you will be able to make well-informed decisions.

Most cloud computing environments are built from thousands of generic computers clustered together. Through clustering and virtualization software, individual computer blades can be added to increase capacity. Clouds, because of the massive redundancy and clustering, are very fault tolerant. If any given component fails, the cluster just works around it. Cloud infrastructure is all about making many different discrete computers work together as an organic whole. Just as living organisms don't depend on any given cell, cloud-based computer infrastructure continues to function as individual components fail and are replaced; clouds grow in power as more components are added.

▶ A "CLOUDY" VIEW OF THE FUTURE

Let's paint a picture of cloud computing as it might be fully realized at some point in the not-too-distant future. You switch on your computer and it powers on instantly to a web browser. Computers of all sizes—notebooks, netbooks, tablets, and smartphones—are optimized for software delivered through the web. Personal computers have no need for local storage, because all data are stored up in the cloud. Gone are the days of installing software on your computer, managing new versions and updates. You do your work on applications accessed via the web.

Beyond a web browser, optimized for fast performance and loaded with plug-ins to handle all kinds of content, there's no need to have any software installed on most computers. By storing all content in the cloud and delivering all software as services, computing becomes more portable and flexible than the days when everything was tied to specific hardware devices. Computer crashes no longer mean a worrisome ordeal of restoring the operating system, reinstalling software, and hoping that your last backup is reasonably up-to-date.

Ubiquitous Internet connectivity means uninterrupted access to all your data and applications. Your collection of music, movies, and video streams in your personal storage space in the cloud is easily accessed from any of your many devices. Likewise, the library's media collection, including thousands of digitized images, documents, videos, and the like reside in high-capacity storage, replicated in multiple ways to protect these irreplaceable objects even if one of your providers suffers some kind of catastrophic technical or business failure.

Cloud computing also reshapes the way that organizations handle their computing needs. Technology infrastructure will become highly specialized to support connectivity and less for storage and computation. There's no need for servers in the library's computer room, for example, because all of its software and systems are accessed via remote services. The integrated library system and other specialized applications are accessed through software-as-a-service arrangements. The library's website and other administrative software are supplied from different service providers. Cloud computing can potentially enable a reality where libraries spend more of their resources creating innovative services without having to worry about the logistics and management of technical infrastructure.

► EVOLVING TOWARD CLOUD COMPUTING TODAY

More realistically, the age of cloud computing hasn't quite arrived in full. Obstacles remain. Internet connectivity, for example, isn't yet sufficiently pervasive or cheap enough for many of us to untether ourselves from local data and software. There are still too many areas without wireless or even cellular data access. Even in well-connected areas, there will always be outages or circumstances where Internet access is problematic. When completely reliant on cloud-based services, interruptions in connectivity mean lost productivity.

Today, cloud computing usually supplements rather than replaces locally installed software. Only a small proportion of organizations have fully implemented cloud-based computing. Yet many organizations have shifted selected aspects of their operations away from locally supported computing, with many planning increased adoption.

Though the trend toward cloud computing is heading upward, traditional local computing still dominates in most libraries. While it's not a given that all computing will shift to the cloud, there are many cloud and cloud-like services already available, with more individuals and organizations adopting this approach. It's fairly easy to take advantage of products and services offered through the cloud for personal use, but moving larger-scale applications from locally supported arrangements to cloud services will take a great deal of planning and maneuvering. We will cover the planning issues more extensively in Chapter 3.

► THE MANY FORMS OF CLOUD COMPUTING

Some cloud-based services come fully formed. Applications such as word processors, spreadsheets, and calendars are often available for little or no cost by simply signing up for an account. You can also use cloud services to create your own customized applications. It's possible to run web servers, databases, and other applications out on a cloud without ever having to purchase your own hardware. Core automation systems such as the integrated library system can be implemented through server arrangements where the vendor hosts and maintains the software.

Cloud computing has become so pervasive that people use it all the time without necessarily realizing it. The popular applications provided by Google for e-mail, word processing, and calendar embody many of the characteristics of cloud computing. See Chapter 7 for practical examples of cloud computing in action.

Although cloud computing has been around a while, we can anticipate ever wider adoption, and it may grow at some point in the near future to be the dominant model for computing. According to Forrester Research, the cloud computing industry will grow from its current size of $41 billion in revenue seen in 2010 to $241 billion in 2020 (see Stefan Ried's April 21, 2011, blog post "Sizing the Cloud" at http://blogs.forrester.com/stefan_ried/11-04-21-sizing_the_cloud).

▶ CONTRASTING EXAMPLE: LOCAL COMPUTING

To understand cloud computing, let's first review the traditional approach, as might apply to your library's web server. It runs on a server that the library owns and maintains, mounted in a rack in a computer center or computer room. You can see it and touch it. Someone's responsible for keeping the operating system up-to-date, configuring the software, and performing other technical and administrative chores. Your library paid the cost of the server hardware and pays for the electricity that powers and cools it.

By contrast cloud computing takes a much more abstract form. It's a service that appears as needed. The hardware on which it resides isn't of direct concern to those who use the service. You're aware it exists somewhere out in the cloud, but where it's located isn't a concern.

Cloud computing is elastic. It isn't of fixed size. Rather, it expands and contracts according to demand. With conventional local computing, if the usage of the computer exceeds the capacity of a server, you have to buy more memory, disk drives, or even more servers. Cloud computing, by contrast, offers the ability to scale computing resources according to variable levels of demand. Capacity fluctuates according to demand, with more computing power available during peaks of high use and scaling down during periods of lower activity. You budget for the computing cycles and storage actually used rather than having to pay for capacity to handle highest use all the time.

▶ A UTILITY MODEL OF COMPUTING

Cloud computing can be characterized as a utility model. There may be some minimum base charge, but what you use is measured, there is a certain cost per unit, and you are billed for what you use. In the same way that the electric company installs a meter that measures what you use and sends you a monthly bill, many forms of cloud computing measure what you use as the basis for what you pay. The more you (or your users) consume, the more you pay. In an infrastructure-as-a-service model, for example, the provider tracks the resources consumed, such as the quantity of virtual servers provisioned; the number of processor cycles, database transactions, bytes stored, and webpages requested; and the incoming or outgoing network activity. Different rates will apply depending on options selected, such as the number of processor cores associated with virtual servers, memory allocated, storage replications, and other factors. Subscription agreements to these services include tables that specify what rates apply to each category of use. The monthly bill will vary depending on usage patterns.

In general terms, cloud computing allows an individual or organization to pay for only the computing resources they use without having to make large up-front purchases for equipment. The fees will increase as any given application gains popularity and will decrease during periods of slack activity. This pay-as-you-go model differs significantly from the budget models that apply to applications implemented on purchased equipment.

Many cloud-based services offer free introductory packages. A variety of consumer-oriented cloud storage sites allow limited amounts of storage either through an advertising-supported business model or as a lead-in to premium paid services. Even higher-end cloud computing environments offer try-before-you-buy options that provide access to a limited amount of computing resources for an introductory period before monthly charges apply. These introductory offers allow an organization to evaluate competing services prior to making a financial commitment to any given offering.

The measured service model to cloud computing can support a low-cost software development environment. The level of computing resources needed and the consumption levels will be much lower during a software development process than they will be once the completed application is placed into production. The general character of cloud computing of paying only for the resources used should result in flexibility and savings compared to the alternative of purchasing equipment that may never be used to its complete potential.

▶ BENEFITS

A number of factors drive the movement toward cloud computing. This approach offers opportunities for organizations to lower their overall costs for technology, improve performance of highly used services, support widely distributed users, and increase reliability.

For many organizations, local computing involves high cost and low efficiency. Even though prices have declined over recent years, server hardware represents a major expense. The capacity of most servers greatly exceeds the current needs of the organization. Because this equipment must last for five or more years, organizations tend to purchase excess capacity beyond immediate needs to accommodate anticipated growth in use. With cloud computing you pay for what you use as you use it instead of paying for excess capacity never consumed.

Personnel costs related to technology can be greatly reduced through increased reliance on cloud computing. Local computing depends on technical personnel with specialized training in server administration, network security, and applications support. The maintenance of local servers involves constant diligence in keeping operating systems on the latest versions, applying security patches on a regular schedule, tuning servers for optimum performance, monitoring systems availability, as well as implementing customizations and configuration changes. Shifting to software delivered through a cloud model can drastically reduce technology-related personnel costs or at least allow an organization to target the talents of their staff members more selectively.

The cloud computing model eliminates the need to purchase and maintain local server hardware. Other than this direct cost component, it impacts indirect costs such as the energy required to power and cool this equipment, any occupancy costs associated with data centers, and administrative overhead.

The business models associated with cloud computing avoid the large up-front costs associated with software licenses. Rather than purchasing permanent licenses, many organizations can achieve substantial savings by shifting to software-as-a-service or other services. Software-as-a-service, for example, usually involves a set monthly or annual subscription fee rather than a large up-front investment for purchasing a license. Traditional software licenses will often require ongoing payments for service and support. The software component of cloud computing may or may not see substantial changes relative to traditional licensing but has the potential to substantially reduce costs related to personnel and hardware.

In Chapter 3, we'll take a closer look at all the cost issues involved, with comparisons between local computing and cloud-based alternatives. It's essential to perform an analysis of total cost of ownership over time in order to understand the budget impact of cloud computing as the basis of an organization's technology strategy.

As libraries more than ever face the need to fulfill their missions with ever few resources, cloud computing can contribute an important dimension to technology strategies. Libraries need to have every possible tool available to them. In the absence of diminishing technical personnel and smaller budgets for computing equipment, it may be possible to gain access to equal or even superior automation products through cloud-based services. In broad terms, increased adoption of cloud services should allow a library to focus its technology budget and personnel less on activities that involve necessary, but routine support for library operations, allowing it to focus more on creating strategic or innovative services. Are there routine support services, such as e-mail, word processing, or financial systems, that the library currently spends excessive time and resources supporting that could be accessed with significantly less effort and expense through some cloud-based service? Does a library want its most technically proficient—and highest paid—personnel spending their time dealing with the upkeep of a room full of servers, or should this talent be focused on higher level activities that make a stronger impact on the library's mission? The subsequent chapters of this book should help clarify the realm of cloud computing from a vague marketing term into a menu of strategic tools for your library.

▶2

TYPES OF SOLUTIONS AVAILABLE

- ▶ **Consider Local Departmental Computing**
- ▶ **Investigate Different Hosting Options**
- ▶ **Move into the Realm of Cloud Computing**
- ▶ **Understand the Pros and Cons of Cloud Computing**

In this chapter we will move beyond the hype associated with cloud computing and take a detailed look at the range of major options for technology infrastructure. We begin by refreshing our memory regarding the characteristics of local computing in order to provide points of comparison with the domain of cloud computing and its many flavors. We then look at some of the hosting arrangements that begin to take libraries away from the realm of local control of computing, finally arriving at the services that more properly reside in the realm of cloud computing.

Today the term "cloud computing" pervades all aspects of discourse about technology, from the scholarly and professional press, to conference presentations, and especially to the promotional materials for products and services. It's become a buzzword and marketing tag loosely applied to a wide range of technical implementation and deployment arrangements. Many different products tend to be promoted through such catch phrases as "in the cloud" without necessarily clarifying the exact technical infrastructure involved. Some of these claims turn out to be more cloud-like than others.

This chapter will step through the various models of computing that tend to be classified as cloud computing either by formal or informal criteria. We will look at some of the broad characteristics encompassed within the realm of cloud computing and the major deployment options. Armed with this information, one can better evaluate the different technology options regardless of the marketing language used to promote specific products and services.

How an organization implements its computing environment can be thought of as a set of implementation options that vary across a spectrum of abstraction. At one end of that spectrum is the traditional model of local computing where one can see and touch all the components involved. At the other extreme are the most abstract models, such as software-as-a-service or platform-as-a-service. In between we see many different alternatives. While there are many different flavors of computing meant by "in the cloud," none of them relates to the tangible equipment that you can see and touch, but all involve some kind of remote or abstract service.

► CONSIDER LOCAL DEPARTMENTAL COMPUTING

First, consider the computing model with the characteristics with the strongest contrast to cloud computing. If your library maintains some or all of its servers that support its automation systems within its own building, it can be thought of as following the model of departmental computing. Many libraries may have a modest data center that houses all of its information technology equipment, including servers, storage arrays, routers, and network switches. This is a style of computing that you can see and touch, where the library has full ownership, control, and responsibility for the infrastructure from the ground up.

This infrastructure isn't necessarily just the computers themselves. Such a data center would also house lots of support equipment, such as individual uninterruptible power supplies for each server, or have a larger enterprise class UPS to support all the equipment. Because computers produce so much heat, special cooling equipment will be needed to maintain reasonable operating temperatures. In many cases the cost of power and cooling equipment can represent as much of an investment as the computing equipment, and the ongoing costs in terms of increased utility bills can't be absent from cost calculations.

Some smaller libraries may have one or two servers that may reside in an office environment, such as in a systems department, and have more modest facilities overhead, but they may likewise not gain the benefits that server-class equipment really need for nonstop reliability and speedy performance. Midsized or larger libraries are more likely to purchase rack-mount computers that take less space, can be more easily managed, and are housed in data closets or a library computer room with more robust environmental controls.

In addition to the physical facilities, the equipment housed in a departmental computer closet or data center requires the attention of technical personnel. Computer technicians, server administrators, or other trained personnel will be involved to install, configure, and maintain this equipment and to deal with problems as they happen.

Departmental computing offers several advantages. If the data center resides within the library, outages of the Internet connection or problems on the broader organization's network may not impact access between staff workstations and the integrated library system (ILS), leaving critical business functions such as circulation and online catalog functions intact. This arrangement also gives the library the highest degree of control in the way that applications are implemented and in priorities of service. When a problem occurs, the library's own staff can take remedial action without having to wait on institutional or external personnel to respond.

On the other hand, the model of departmental computing imposes the highest level of responsibility on the library and the highest cost. The library must absorb the full cost of purchasing the equipment, maintaining a suitable operating environment, and providing the requisite personnel resources. Equipment needs to be replaced every few years, resulting in an endless cycle of procurement, installation, and maintenance. The library's own personnel need to be on call at all times to deal with any interruptions in service that would have a negative impact on the operations of the library. These high thresholds of investment and cost have been key drivers in exploring alternatives to this approach to library computing in favor of other more enterprise-oriented and ultimately cloud-based models.

▶ INVESTIGATE DIFFERENT HOSTING OPTIONS

Remote Website Hosting

Many libraries rely on institutional or commercial hosting services for their websites. In this case, the library isn't leasing an entire server but running its website through a hosting service. The library does not have to get involved with the hardware that supports the site but will contract for the service based on the number of pages involved, the bandwidth consumed, or other usage-based factors. Such a service might simply host pages as developed by the library, but many will provide consulting and design services and other assistance needed to create a professional presentation and organizational structure.

It's common for a library's web presence to be provided not directly by the library itself but by its parent organization. Especially in a university setting, the library might participate in an enterprise content management system rather than operate its own web server.

Some of the considerations of using an external website hosting service include the library's ability to run different kinds of scripting languages that might be needed for special features, support of content management systems such as Drupal or Joomla, and whether the library is able to directly access the files of the site to perform updates.

The operation of a library's website falls into the realm of the many aspects of technology in transition from complete local ownership and control toward enterprise-oriented or more abstract provision of its underlying infrastructure.

Server Colocation

Given the high costs of maintaining their own departmental computing facilities, many libraries enter arrangements to outsource the physical housing of their server infrastructure with some external provider. Libraries within larger organizations, such as colleges, universities, research facilities, medical centers, hospitals, corporations, municipal or county governments, and the like may be able to take advantage of larger-scale, consolidated data centers that provide technical infrastructure for all their units or departments in addition to the infrastructure they maintain on behalf of the organization as a whole. The movement from departmental to enterprise computing has been one of the major information technology trends of the past two decades. Having each department within an organization house its own computing infrastructure is much less efficient than relying on more sophisticated and robust, industrial-strength services for the entire organization. Having one centralized e-mail service for the whole organization, for example, offers far more efficiency than multiple departmental servers. An enterprise data center will operate applications such as finance, payroll, e-mail, or other communications service that benefit the entire organization. In addition, most of these data centers house, and at least partially operate, specialized servers and services on behalf of units and departments throughout the organization. In this vein, campus data centers routinely house the servers for a library's automation system.

In most colocation arrangements, the library would continue to have ownership and some degree of responsibility for the server. A typical arrangement might involve the central IT staff taking responsibility for physical hardware maintenance and operating system issues, with the library assuming responsibility for software applications, such as the ILS, digital asset management environment, or other library-specific applications.

It is also possible for libraries to take advantage of colocation arrangements with external commercial providers. Libraries that don't want to house their own servers but are not part of a larger organization can contract with external hosting companies to house their equipment in industrial-strength data centers.

Server colocation represents the first step away from local computing to more abstract approaches. It essentially outsources the housing and upkeep of the hardware to an external entity. Although the hardware is "out of sight," it is not "out of mind," however, because it continues to require technical management by the library.

Dedicated Server Hosting

A similar approach involves contracting for the use of a server from an institutional or commercial data center. In this arrangement, the data center owns the equipment and provides exclusive use of it for a set price per month or year. Dedicated server hosting eliminates the up-front costs of purchasing the hardware. The customer, such as a library contracting for a server to host its ILS, retains full control over the administration of the operating system and applications. The cost of a dedicated server may also vary according to the operating system provided. It is more expensive, for example, to contract for a server running a commercial operating system such as Microsoft Windows Server, where the license fees must be amortized, than for open source options such as Linux.

In a dedicated server hosting environment, the library has exclusive control of the server equipment. Only applications installed by the library will run on it, possibly with the exception of management modules that the hosting facility might want to install to ensure its optimal operation. Access to the server for administration would be accomplished through tools such as a secure shell for Linux- or Unix-based systems or through Remote Desktop or Remotely Anywhere for Windows servers.

From an operational perspective, a dedicated server hosting arrangement resembles colocation arrangements. The key difference is the business model whereby colocation involves equipment owned by the customer and dedicated hosting essentially leases servers provided by the provider. Dedicated hosting tends to involve external commercial providers rather than institutional data centers.

In a dedicated hosting arrangement, end-user access to the application travels through the provider's Internet connectivity rather than the library's. In most cases this arrangement results in much higher bandwidth capacity to the server than would be the case if this traffic passed through the library's network. Because access by library personnel passes through the Internet instead of the local network, some concerns may apply to the security of the connections, which can be resolved through the use of a VPN (virtual private network).

Dedicated hosting makes sense when the library needs full control of the server and a highly reliable environment. A commercial hosting company can offer a more secure environment with many layers of redundancy for power, cooling, and Internet connectivity than a library would be able to within its own facilities. Dedicated hosting may be a reasonable alternative for custom-developed applications or for proprietary or open source products not offered through software-as-a-service, as described later.

Virtual Server Hosting

Moving toward more abstract models of computing, a library may be able to run its applications on a virtualized server rather than a dedicated server. In this case, the library gains access to an instance of an operating environment that may coexist on a server with other instances. In other words, the library gets access to a full running version of an operating environment but does not gain exclusive access to the hardware upon which it runs.

Virtual hosting can be considerably less expensive than dedicated server hosting. Because the provider can let out multiple virtual servers for each physical server, its overhead is substantially lower. To take advantage of the lower costs of virtual server hosting over a dedicated server, the applications involved must be well-tested for a virtualized environment, and the processing required should be below the threshold that requires a dedicated server to satisfy.

Both virtual server hosting and dedicated server hosting tend to be priced at a fixed rate per month or per year and not variable according to use levels as we will see later for the offerings more properly associated with cloud computing.

► MOVE INTO THE REALM OF CLOUD COMPUTING

Infrastructure-as-a-Service

As we consider the differing models of computer infrastructure deployment, infrastructure-as-a-service, often abbreviated IaaS, falls within what would more legitimately be considered cloud computing. This model breaks away from thinking of computing in terms of specific servers toward a more flexible and abstract approach to gaining the right level of capacity for an organization's technical infrastructure.

IaaS involves subscribing to computing and storage capabilities on an as-needed basis. This model differs from the dedicated or virtual server hosting models in that the allocation and pricing of the computing resources vary by actual consumption rather than fixed monthly fees. IaaS allows an organization to gain access to computing resources—such as an instance of Linux or Windows—scaled to the demands and duration of a project. A short-term development task, for example, can be accomplished at minimal cost. The environment of major production systems can be built on IaaS, deployed on computing resources appropriately scaled in terms of number of processors, memory available per processor, disk storage capacity and services such as geographic replication, or disaster recovery options.

With IaaS, the organization will never see the physical hardware involved, but will perform much of the systems administration tasks as they would for local servers. Operating an application through IaaS saves the organization from the purchase of its own hardware, eliminates the overhead associated with the maintenance of hardware, but retains the tasks associated with installing and maintaining software applications.

Resources allocated to an application can be increased and decreased according to anticipated use. This "elastic" characteristic of IaaS ensures adequate capacity during peak periods with the ability to step down allocated resources should use levels fall. When an organization delivers an application through IaaS, it pays for only the computing resources it uses, with much more flexibility than would apply to locally owned equipment or dedicated or virtual hosting arrangements.

IaaS can be deployed for many different kinds of scenarios: development and production environment for custom-developed software, platform for implementing licensed commercial software, or open source applications. A library might use IaaS to operate its ILS, for example, rather than purchase local hardware. An ILS vendor might use IaaS as the infrastructure to support its software-as-a-service or application service provider offerings.

Exploration or implementation of infrastructure services can be phased in gradually. Organizations that base their computing environment on local computing equipment might consider implementing some aspect of supplemental resources through IaaS. Projects involving custom software, development, prototypes, and testing can take place on resources allocated through IaaS even when the production environment will run on dedicated servers. A development environment can be ramped up and torn down as needed, providing a very inexpensive and flexible way to support a library's research and development efforts. Copies of data, programming code, and configuration files can reside on more persistent storage allocations, even when computing resources have been set aside. This approach provides a flexible way for programmers to have access to computing resources, without having to deal with all the technical and procedural overhead involved in procuring, installing, and maintaining local hardware. Although there are many other providers, Amazon.com ranks as one of the most popular providers of IaaS. It's Elastic Compute Cloud, or EC2, service provides access to either Windows or Linux computing instances delivered through Amazon Machine Images. When procuring this service, the customer specifies such things as whether to use Windows or Linux as the operating system and to select from a range of memory and processor options, with prices per hour scaled accordingly.

Data Storage in the Cloud

In the current environment, devices and equipment for storing data have become incredibly inexpensive and flexible. USB-attached disk drives with capacities of up to 3 TB are now available for today for around $250, and 16 GB flash drives can be purchased for around $20. Given the incredible amounts of storage available at such little cost, is there a need for storage delivered through the cloud?

Although storage options based on tangible local devices may be inexpensive and flexible in lots of ways, they also have disadvantages. USB flash drives can easily be misplaced and are inherently insecure. Few users of these devices bother to perform file encryption or employ other techniques to prevent anyone who comes across a misplaced device from accessing files. Misplacing one of these devices can result in a sensitive file leaking beyond its intended audience or not having a copy of your presentation files when you need them for an important speech.

Keep in mind the inherent fragility of all physical storage devices. They can fail at any time and can be lost or destroyed by unforeseen events. The data on the internal drive in your laptop or desktop computer can be lost through hardware failures, software malfunctions, malware attacks, or through human error. It's essential to have many copies of any computer file of importance.

The utmost care needs to be given to both personal and organizational data. Anyone would feel devastated to lose personal files such as family photos, financial information, genealogy research, or other kinds of information that represented untold hours of work to create. Most individuals and organizations think about and plan for what physical items might be lost in a fire, flood, burglary, or other major incident. It's also important to think about our digital assets. If all the computing equipment in your home were stolen or destroyed, would you be able to recover all your files from copies stored elsewhere? One of the basic strategies for data security involves keeping multiple copies spread across multiple geographic locations. Having all the copies of digital assets in your home doesn't offer adequate protection. Keeping an extra copy at your office or at a friend's or relative's place is better; having a copy in a distant city is even better.

Placing copies of data on physical devices stored in different geographic locations can be an inconvenient process, especially when it comes to keeping all the copies up-to-date. Every time you add a batch of new photos, for example, you would need to find a way to get copies onto the drives you have in remote locations. Cloud-based storage can be used to address the vulnerabilities inherent in relying solely on physical devices for important digital assets.

IaaS involves storing files and data through an external provider. Cloud-based storage, sometimes called storage-as-a-service, represents a major component of IaaS. These services accommodate many different types of use, ranging from casual personal use to large-scale mission critical enterprise implementations. Storage services can be used in association with full-blown applications deployed through IaaS, as a backup mechanism for locally hosted applications, as a means to transfer data from one individual or organization to another, or as a temporary work space for a project. Just about any activity that involves either short-term or long-term storage of data can take advantage of storage delivered through the cloud for flexible access and often with less expense than purchasing local storage.

Amazon's Simple Storage Service, or S3, provides disk storage through a web service. The configuration of the storage, involving factors such as the level of redundancy and backup services provided, will impact the unit costs and expected reliability and disaster recovery possibilities. Data related to mission-critical services can be allocated storage with more redundancy and services than would be needed for temporary storage of data where primary copies exist elsewhere. Environments based on EC2 will likely use S3 for storage of data and program files. It's also very common to use S3 independently for projects that benefit from cloud-based storage but are accessed in other ways. S3, while protecting data as private by default, can also be configured to share files either to other users of the Amazon Web Services or as widely as needed through enabling access by publishing them to the web.

Addressing the Need for Personal Portable Storage

Many data storage services are geared toward personal users, offering modest amounts of space at little or no cost. These services provide a very convenient way for individuals to have portable access to their files and to share data with others. These are a few such services:

▶ **Dropbox** (http://www.dropbox.com/) offers a free 2 GB storage option, with installable client drivers that make the service appear as any other folder. Dragging files into the folder automatically initiates transfer to Dropbox, which can then be shared with other users. Dropbox is a convenient way for an individual to share files among multiple computers (Windows, Mac, Linux) and mobile devices (iPhone, iPad, Android, BlackBerry).

> ► **Windows Live SkyDrive** (http://explore.live.com/windows-live-skydrive) offers free storage up to 25 GB, geared primarily to users of Microsoft Windows for use with the Office suite of business applications. Once uploaded to SkyDrive, documents can be edited directly on Microsoft's web-based Office Live or Office 365 applications or with Office applications installed on a user's workstation. SkyDrive can be used as a backup copy as a contingency against problems with those stored on a hard drive of a laptop or desktop computer. As with other cloud storage services, documents stored on SkyDrive are available only when the user is connected to the Internet. This limitation requires users to rely on local documents when connectivity is not available.
> ► **Amazon Cloud Drive** (https://www.amazon.com/clouddrive/learnmore) currently allows free storage of up to 5 GB of files. It is positioned to deliver a cloud-based music service with Amazon's Cloud Player.
> ► **Box.net** (http://www.box.net/) is a cloud storage provider mostly oriented to businesses, which also includes a free personal storage service up to 5 GB.
> ► **ADrive** (http://www.adrive.com/) provides up to 50 GB free storage for personal use, supported by third-party advertisements. The company's premium services target business with enterprise storage needs up to 10 TB.

Cloud storage services provide a very convenient way to deal with all of the files and data that pervade our personal and work lives. For personal files, free storage services allow one to have multiple copies of files to reduce the odds of losing important information, usually the products of hours of work. Given the current abundance of free services, it would be a good strategy to make copies of files on one or two cloud storage services in addition to the copies held on a laptop or desktop computer.

Cloud storage services can also be used for work-related files, but it's important to be sure that this use is consistent with the expectations of your employer. Most libraries provide shared drives on file servers where they expect personnel to store their documents. These shared network drives can be configured to provide shared access to the teams, work groups, or committees to facilitate collaboration. If individuals within these teams instead place their files on a separate cloud-based service, it may disrupt the processes and procedures established for the organization. If these kinds of services are not provided in the work environment, then cloud services may be an approach to consider for establishing them.

But it's important to be aware of their limitations as well as their benefits— one should not become overly reliant on any given service. You cannot expect a free service to take any responsibility for your data. If you lose your username or password, accidently delete files, or lose data through any other kind of technical mishap, you cannot expect the service to recover the account or restore your files. These are the kinds of features offered with the paid premium services of the cloud storage providers. Likewise, even if the loss is due to a failure of the provider, the provider may not be under any obligation to protect or restore your files. Most importantly, be prepared for the service to go out of business or for the withdrawal of free services in favor of paid accounts. Although it seems likely that free services will continue to prosper, they should be treated as a convenience, not as the sole basis for preserving important assets.

Given the importance of protecting individual or institutional data, it's essential to implement a strategy that delivers an adequate level of protection. Such a strategy might include a combination of local and cloud-based storage, synchronizing copies across multiple independent cloud services, or subscribing to cloud services with multiple layers of disaster recovery services. For institutional data, be sure to consult and collaborate with the organization's IT department to ensure that your use of cloud services complements and does not contradict their efforts to ensure efficient, reliable, and secure treatment of your organization's data assets.

Software-as-a-Service

One of the most popular forms of cloud computing today involves the access to software applications over the web rather than using individual instances installed on a local workstation or provided through an organization's servers. This model of computing provides access to all features and functionality of an application without having to be involved in the technical details of how it is hosted. In its purest form, users access the application through a web browser, with all the data involved stored on the provider's servers.

Applications delivered through the software-as-a-service (SaaS) model ideally follow a multitenant architecture. This characteristic involves the ability for a single instance of the application to be shared among many different organizations or individual users simultaneously. All users of the software might be able to configure the software for their specific needs, and their data will be partitioned appropriately. Whether the SaaS application is geared toward organizations or individual users, layers of authentication and authorization in conjunction with appropriate data architectures ensure that each tenant of the application gains access to its full functionality with complete assurance that others will not gain unauthorized access to their data. SaaS can also be used in collaborative ways when users explicitly elect to share data.

SaaS offers a much more efficient approach relative to traditional locally installed software both for the provider and for the consumer. These efficiencies have driven the software industry toward this deployment model, although many legacy applications remain—especially in the library automation arena.

From the provider's perspective, there is just one instance of the software to support, operating on a single platform. Enhancements and bug fixes can be implemented once for all customers. While the scale of the platform comes with its own challenges and complications, much smaller levels of effort are needed to support each organization or individual customer. With traditional software, whether hosted by the vendor in an application service provider arrangement or on the customer's premises, upgrades must be installed for each of these separate instances. The complexity increases as different customer sites may operate the software on different brands and configurations of hardware, under different operating systems, and even with local customizations that confound routine upgrade and support issues.

From the consumer's perspective, SaaS eliminates multiple layers of technical support, because it requires no local server hardware, no software installed on each end-user computer, and no technical administration of operating systems, database engines, or other infrastructure components. SaaS shifts much of the responsibility for maintaining an application from the organization to the provider. Version updates, patches, enhancements, and other changes to the software appear automatically rather than having to be installed by the customer. The traditional software deployment model, because of the great effort involved, often results in libraries operating software years out of date and thus not being able to access current features, bug fixes, and security patches.

One of the classic examples of an SaaS targeting organizational implementations is Salesforce.com (http://www.salesforce.com/), a customer relationship management (CRM) platform used by many tens of thousands of companies and other organizations worldwide to manage their sales and support activities. It stands as the epitome of cloud computing. Organizations that subscribe to Salesforce.com create a customized environment that provides a comprehensive environment for tracking customers, automates the sales process, and offers a dashboard of metrics and analytics that measure the performance of the company in each of its activities. Salesforce.com also offers its own platform-as-a-service, Force.com (http://force.com/), that organizations can use to build their own custom applications.

The library automation arena continues to be dominated by traditional software designed to be implemented for individual libraries or consortia. Only some of the more recent products have been designed and deployed through SaaS. Serials Solutions, for example, offers its products exclusively in an SaaS model, including its 360 Suite of products for management and access to electronic resources and its Summon discovery service. Many of the new generation library automation products are being designed for SaaS, including Primo Central and Alma from Ex Libris. Yet the majority of the library automation products available today were created prior to the time when cloud computing concepts such as multitenant SaaS entered the technology scene. See Chapter 3 for a more detailed treatment of the library automation products and services based on cloud technologies.

The payment model for SaaS varies depending on many factors, including whether it is intended for personal or institutional use. Commercial business applications, such as major library automation systems, would be made available through a monthly or annual subscription fee. The terms of a subscription to an SaaS offering would specify such things as what customer support will be provided, guaranteed availability, and other details. The cost of the subscription will be set according to consumption factors, such as modules or options deployed, numbers of monthly transactions, or as monthly or annual charges based on the size and complexity of the organization or the potential number of users in the organization.

Many of the most popular productivity or communications applications, either in the context of personal or business use, are accessed through SaaS. Obvious examples include Gmail and Google Docs. Users consume these applications through their web browsers, with no local software

An increasing number of applications originally offered as locally installed software are transitioning to SaaS or other cloud-based delivery models. Examples include Microsoft's Office 365, a cloud-based SaaS, mentioned earlier, that provides similar functionality to the Office suite of productivity applications designed to be installed on individual computers. In the personal and small business finance realm, products such as Intuit's QuickBooks have evolved from software installed on individual computers to also being offered as web-based services, as has its TurboTax tax preparation software.

Organizations involved in creating products offered through a SaaS often depend on other providers to host their applications. It's possible, or even likely, that a company offering a library automation system through an SaaS will deploy the software using computing resources through an IaaS provider such as Amazon.com, provisioning the requisite number of server images and storage through EC2 and S3, or might contract with a major server hosting facility such as Rackspace. Organizations with core expertise in software development and support are not necessarily the ones best positioned to deliver highly reliable infrastructure services.

Application Service Provider

The concept of using software applications via the Internet is not especially recent, with many software firms offering their products in hosted arrangements since the 1990s through an arrangement called "application service provider," or ASP. This deployment model relies on the server component of a business application to be hosted by a vendor—usually the company that developed the software—rather than at the customer's site. In the era of client/server computing, the standard configuration consisted of the server component installed in the data center of an organization, accessed by graphical clients installed on the computers of end users. In the context of an ILS, for example, the library operates the server component, with specialized Windows, Macintosh, or Java clients installed on the workstations of any personnel who operate the system. Library users access the public catalog of the system through a web browser. The traditional client/server application includes a server component installed in the library, specialized clients for library personnel, and web-based online catalog for library patrons; each instance of the server application supports a single library or consortium.

In the ASP arrangement, all aspects of the client/server deployment remain the same, but the server component resides in a data center operated by the software provider and the clients access that server through the Internet instead of the local network. The provider maintains individual instances of the server component that correspond to each library or consortium making use of the product.

This model of software deployment provides many of the characteristics of SaaS for legacy applications not specifically designed for multitenant access. It offers significant benefits for libraries, or other organizations, taking advantage of the service, though it imposes higher thresholds of effort for the providers of the service.

From the perspective of the library, most of the benefits of SaaS apply, such as relief from the maintenance of local hardware and the technical details of administering the operating system and software applications, as well as the budget model of fixed subscription pricing rather than variable local technical and personnel expenses. This model does not provide relief in dealing with the specialized clients associated with the applications. In the context of the ILS, the graphical clients continue to need to be installed on each staff workstation, replete with the requirement to install upgrades and maintain the configuration details for each workstation. The option to deploy through ASP naturally depends on the library having sufficient Internet bandwidth to support the traffic between the staff and end-user clients and the vender-hosted server.

From the perspective of the vendor, the ASP model requires much more effort than would a multitenant SaaS environment. The vendor must maintain individual instances of the server application for each customer site, including all configuration selections, policy parameters, database tables, and other complexities. Through virtualization and other techniques that allow for large-scale consolidation of computing resources, an ASP can achieve much greater efficiencies than would apply to individual installations at customer sites, though still falling short of the full benefits of multitenant SaaS. Table 2.1 compares the SaaS and ASP models.

It is common for products delivered through what might more correctly be considered ASP to be marketed as SaaS. It is reasonable to consider ASP as a subset of the broader concept of SaaS, but a library should be well-informed regarding the issues described in this section.

Platform-as-a-Service

Organizations that create custom applications can take advantage of a platform-as-a-service (PaaS), which offers a complete development and production environment, abstracted from concerns with details of underlying infrastructure. Such a platform would offer a complete technology stack, including support for a programming language or applications programming interface, database functionality, data stores, computational resources, and other components needed to create a complete web-based application. A platform will provide a software development kit, or SDK, to provide the documentation that programmers need to create applications. Some of the most well-known PaaS offerings include the following:

▶ **Table 2.1: Features of the Software-as-a-Service and Application Service Provider Models**

Multitenant SaaS	Application Service Provider
One instance serves all organizational or individual users	One instance per organization
All functionality delivered through web-based interfaces	Specialized clients (Windows, Mac, Java)
Data managed by provider	Data managed by provider
Access to application via Internet	Access to application via Internet
Provider administers software and deploys new versions	Provider administers software and deploys new versions
Consumption-based pricing or set subscription fees	Set subscription fees
Service access through the Internet	Service access through the Internet

▶ **Google App Engine** (http://code.google.com/appengine) supports programming languages such as Java, Python, and Go (an open source programming language created by Google).

▶ **Amazon Web Services** (http://aws.amazon.com) includes a complex set of products spanning both IaaS and PaaS.

▶ **Force.com** (http://www.force.com/) is the underlying platform for Salesforce.com that can be used to create custom applications, primarily through a web-based development environment.

▶ **Bungee Connect** (http://www.bungeeconnect.com/) is a platform for the development of cloud-based apps that will be deployed on IaaS such as Amazon's EC2.

▶ **Heroku** (http://www.heroku.com/) is a PaaS for the Ruby programming language, including both development and a fully managed deployment environment.

The realm of PaaS offerings is of interest primarily to individuals or organizations that develop web-based applications. This approach can also be used to create add-ons to existing applications. Many library developers, for example, have written utilities and extensions making use of OCLC's WorldShare Platform as a development platform. Building on top of a PaaS not only simplifies development by avoiding the need for programmers to deal with operating system and infrastructure issues but also results in highly scalable and robust applications with inherent cloud-computing characteristics.

▶ UNDERSTAND THE PROS AND CONS OF CLOUD COMPUTING

While cloud computing offers a method of computing with a number of advantages, it comes with issues and limitations that a library must take into consideration as it considers increased involvement. No technology can be expected to offer only positive traits. Any negative characteristics need to be understood up-front so that even if the balance leans toward adopting the technology the appropriate measures are taken to mitigate risk and maximize advantages.

Security Issues

In general, concerns for security and privacy should be considered neutral when comparing cloud computing with local systems management. The same types of tools and techniques are available across both environments for ensuring tight security. The same lapses in security can take place under either approach. Through IaaS offerings, such as Amazon's EC2, libraries can be assured of working with the instances of operating systems replete with the latest security patches. One of the significant advantages of cloud services lies in the provider taking responsibility for software and operating system updates. These providers have a great deal at stake in avoiding the kinds of embarrassing issues that would arise from security breaches that might be caused through offering instances of virtual machines out of date or missing critical security patches.

Taking advantage of cloud services does not eliminate the responsibility for an organization to take reasonable security measures. Password management, proper use of encryption for passing sensitive information, policies against sharing authentication credentials, and other standard security policies and practices apply regardless of the deployment model implemented.

Any custom-developed applications will have basically the same security concerns when operated in an IaaS environment as they would on local hardware. Programmers must code with care to avoid vulnerabilities such as cross-site scripting, SQL injections, or any of the techniques that can be exploited without rigorous defensive measures.

Security concerns for applications accessed through SaaS will vary relative to the attention the provider pays to these issues. Given the higher stakes and likelihood that an organization offering an SaaS product to a large number of customers would have deep technical resources, including seasoned system administrators and security specialists, libraries should expect a lower level of risk than with local hosting and fewer technical specialists. When procuring major library applications through SaaS, expectations regarding security practices and privacy of data should be clearly understood and incorporated into the terms of the subscription agreement.

Libraries have responsibilities to safeguard the privacy of data. While much of the data that libraries manage is intended to be widely shared, such as the bibliographic databases that describe their collections, some categories must be well-guarded as private, such as personal details of library patrons, the library's personnel records, or certain financial information. It's essential that any cloud-based deployments that involve sensitive data follow the standard practices, such as using SSL (secure sockets layer) for any log-in to accounts that provide access to sensitive data and to encrypt any webpages that present personal details. Organizations such as financial firms, military, or government agencies that deal with classified information, trade secrets, or other highly sensitive data tend to avoid using public cloud implementations that might allow co-mingling of data on a physical infrastructure outside of their direct ownership or control. Such an organization would be more likely to use a local infrastructure or a private cloud environment that partitions an organization's data and computing resources away from that of other tenants.

From a privacy and security perspective, comfort levels for using cloud-based products vary depending on the type of information and activity involved. E-mail, because it involves messages that will be exposed to the Internet anyway, is not an application that causes much concern. Savvy e-mail users know not to send any messages that contain highly sensitive content or to use some kind of encryption as needed. General word processing files, such as student papers, general office correspondence and reports, or professional work, likewise does not trigger a great deal of worry. Standard restrictions through authenticated accounts provide reasonable security and privacy. Personal or institutional financial information, however, tends to invoke a bit more concern. When choosing whether to shift from local applications to a cloud-based service, it's prudent to be sure that the organization is aware and informed and gives consistent attention to the use of externally provided computing resources with any categories of data that might be perceived as sensitive.

Reliability Issues

Libraries, like most organizations, have a low tolerance for interruptions in service. We also tend to have a very high reliance on the integrity of data. The operational, bibliographic, and financial data held within an ILS represents untold hours of effort and would be catastrophic if lost; any interruptions in service can be extremely inconvenient to library patrons and personnel. The data related to a library's digital collection may be unique and irreplaceable.

As with any technology option, cloud computing is vulnerable to failures. While expected levels of reliability may be extremely high, responsible use of cloud computing for mission-critical applications demands a set of disaster recovery plans that would be followed for locally implemented projects.

Cloud-based services have been designed to offer a much higher level of reliability than most organizations can accomplish within their own data centers. Large-scale cloud providers such as Amazon, Google, and Rackspace base their services on an architecture designed to withstand failures. Well-designed cloud services assume that any hardware component will fail and that the requests will be rerouted accordingly with no perceptible interruption in service. The data centers themselves have multiple layers of power protection and other environmental controls to be less vulnerable to local events that affect the availability of electricity. Amazon, for example, offers options where a service may be supported through multiple geographically separated zones to support organizations that must deliver extremely fault-tolerant applications.

Although cloud computing generally delivers much higher levels of reliability than local hosting arrangements, failures do happen. The reputation for the reliability of cloud services became a bit tarnished in April 21, 2011, when Amazon Web Services experienced a major failure that resulted in outages for many products that rely on its infrastructure, including Foursquare, Reddit, Quora, and HootSuite. The outage lasted for the greater part of a day, and many applications experienced longer service interruptions depending on what was needed to restore their operations. This event highlighted that organizations must plan for failures, even when they depend on cloud-based infrastructure. Amazon's customers who took advantage of multi-region deployments, for example, were able to avoid the service interruption.

It's not sufficient to just put your data and application on a cloud-based infrastructure and hope for the best. Cloud services such as Amazon's EC2 offer a wide range of deployment options, allowing organizations to design the appropriate level of contingency plans. In the same manner that one would implement routine data backup procedures for locally hosted applications, the same kinds of considerations apply for any cloud-based implementation. Infrastructure failures can still happen, though with less frequency; vulnerability to errant software events or human error doesn't magically disappear. Stringent data preservation and backup procedures must be designed into any use of cloud services, whether it's for personal use or for your organization.

Fortunately, it's fairly easy to implement backup and contingency plans with cloud services. Many services will offer backup services as an added-cost option. These services will include procedures similar to what an organization would perform for its local servers, such as regular backup copies made to alternate media, such as tape, with the ability to rapidly restore files in the event of failure of the cloud storage system or data corruption through problems with the customer's application software. But these services may significantly increase the storage costs. While raw cloud-based storage can appear on the surface to be quite inexpensive, it's essential to also factor in services for reasonable disaster recovery contingencies.

Another strategy for protecting your data is to place copies on other, separate cloud storage services with regular synchronizing. It's extremely unlikely that failures would take place simultaneously among separate, geographically dispersed storage services. If you rely on multiple storage services, be sure that they are actually separate and not resident on the same physical data centers.

For projects involving a modest amount of data—measured in gigabytes rather than terabytes—strategies involving multiple storage services can be implemented with little expense. The cost of the storage, the bandwidth involved in moving it, or other safety measures may be well below the expense of the components involved for regular backups of locally managed data, such as disk-to-disk backup hardware, tape drives and media, and enterprise backup software.

For an additional measure of safety, libraries may also want to keep local copies of data for projects that involve cloud-based services. For an SaaS ILS deployment, for example, these copies can provide insurance against business failures or contract disputes as much as for technical failures.

For strategies involving duplicate copies of data on alternate cloud services or local storage, some type of automatic process should be implemented to ensure that the backup copies are recent enough to be helpful in the event of a failure. In most cases, scheduled scripts can be implemented to refresh the copies as frequently as needed. The tried-and-true concepts of file management should be applied regardless of the deployment model: full backups made weekly or monthly with daily or hourly incremental backups for changed or modified files.

Most SaaS arrangements for major applications include service-level agreements that specify what actions the provider will implement to protect data. The measures required should meet or exceed the standard practices that a library would follow for locally managed systems. Depending on the level of assurance provided in the service-level agreement and the confidence that the library has in the provider, additional measures may be instituted to receive local copies of data as an added level of protection.

Other cloud-oriented applications, such as e-mail services, may not warrant extensive measures beyond those bundled with the product. Some categories of data would be inconvenient to lose access to for a limited period but would not necessarily result in a major interruption of the library's services.

The library's Internet connectivity can also impact the perceived reliability of the cloud-based services on which it relies. If the library has unstable or inadequate bandwidth, it may not be able to connect to service from external providers, causing interruptions for library personnel and for users within the library, even when remote users can access the services without problems. Robust access to the Internet is one of the key prerequisites of involvement with cloud computing.

On the whole, cloud-based services can offer a much higher level of reliability than most libraries are able to accomplish on their own equipment. Few libraries have the capacity to purchase the hardware necessary to implement the levels of redundancy routinely implemented in major cloud service facilities.

Large-Scale Data

Some libraries deal with very large-scale sets of data, involving many terabytes or even petabytes of content. Large-scale video collections, scientific data sets, or large image collections are a few examples of the library projects that involve immense quantities of data storage.

It's clear that cloud-based services, such as Amazon's S3, can handle data on a very large scale. Yet, there may be practical limitations that may make local storage a better choice. The cost advantages between local storage and cloud storage change dramatically with very large-scale data sets. The 140 TB of storage underlying the Vanderbilt Television News Archive, for example, would incur monthly charges of $16,560, or $198,720 per year, or $993,600 over a five-year period, if stored in the Amazon S3 service. These numbers greatly exceed the costs for purchasing the equipment to provide equivalent storage capacity on the organization's local network.

Another factor in dealing with very large-scale storage involves the time and cost of the bandwidth required for a transfer from its local source to a storage provider. Most storage service providers include charges for incoming and outgoing transfers, though these costs are quite modest compared to storage. The time required for the transfer of very large files can also be prohibitive. While some major universities and research centers have access to very high bandwidth through Internet2, the majority of libraries have more modest connectivity, and routine transfers of large data sets could take hours or days. Recognizing how cumbersome it may be to transfer large amounts of data, Amazon offers a service whereby a customer can ship a physical drive and Amazon will upload its contents into an S3 bucket.

The positive and negative factors balance differently as projects scale up from those that manage mere gigabytes to those that involve dozens or hundreds of terabytes. The positive aspects of increased flexibility, convenient access, and reliability still apply, but the costs can skyrocket and logistical tasks to transfer into and out of the cloud storage services become more challenging. While there may be some cases where a library might find it expedient to use cloud storage for these kinds of projects, current pricing models and bandwidth capacities make it a less viable option.

Environmental Issues

Cloud computing results in a reduced environmental impact through reduced amounts of energy consumed relative to the use of discrete equipment. The cumulative resources consumed by hundreds of servers, as might be operated in a typical university data center, or thousands or tens of thousands, as are routinely managed in commercial data centers, can make a major environmental impact. The consolidation of servers through virtualization, or through more aggressive computer utilization accomplished through cloud computing, results in fewer physical servers and proportional savings in energy consumption.

The use of cloud-based services will reduce consumption of energy resources within the library. Operating fewer servers results in an incremental reduction in power and cooling resources. Fully eliminating a library's data center will make an even more noticeable impact. Greater energy savings are gained through the consolidation of equipment from many smaller data centers to larger facilities with more efficient power utilization, at least on a per-server basis. Transferring servers from a smaller and less energy-efficient computer room in the library to an institutional data center or an external hosting center or cloud service not only reduces the library's energy bills but also energy consumption overall. Reducing power consumption by moving away from less efficient local servers to other less consumptive models can be seen as a positive contribution to an organization's green initiative.

Version Control

When operating locally installed software, keeping applications up-to-date with current versions can be a major challenge. Planning for major software upgrades, or even minor patches, requires intervention of the library's technical personnel. Major functional upgrades that involve new or changed functionality in the way that library personnel use the software or that impacts end-user features may require significant training and testing. Many academic libraries, for example, interested in avoiding disruptions during busy periods, will schedule major updates to take place during breaks in the academic calendar. Major updates can also require higher levels of hardware support, which may exceed the capacity of the library's server equipment. Especially in the realm of ILSs, many libraries operate versions of the software that are many years out of date even when they are entitled to updates through their maintenance or support fees.

SaaS shifts the burden of implementing software updates from the library's local staff to the vendor. Although major updates may still require scheduling, minor updates and patches can be routinely implemented by the vendor across all the customers subscribing to the service. Major updates may require some coordination on scheduling. Because the SaaS provider takes responsibility for the hardware platform, the need to upgrade customer hardware does not apply as it does with local installations.

Flexible Environment for Library Developers

An area where cloud computing really shines lies in the realm of software development. For libraries involved in the creation of custom applications or other tech-heavy projects, cloud-based services can provide many benefits.

Maintaining local computers for development involves considerable effort and expense. Local computers require ongoing cost commitments, from procurement, to maintenance, through replacement. Time investment in dealing with local hardware adds a layer of overhead that detracts from the essential tasks involved in software development. Purchasing and setting up a server for development can take days or weeks to prepare. Ramping up a server instance through an IaaS such as Amazon's EC2 can be done in a matter of minutes. This approach can facilitate the rapid creation of prototypes that, delivered through a cloud service, can be accessed and critiqued from anywhere on the Internet. Cloud-based development can be especially well-suited to distributed development teams that may include members from different institutions around the world. Cloud-based software development can be quite inexpensive, with many library projects falling within thresholds of free service or at least where monthly subscription fees fall well below direct and indirect costs of local equipment. Cloud computing generally offers a very attractive total cost of ownership value, yet projects involving very large-scale data sets fall into a bracket where cloud computing costs greatly exceed local storage options. Unless the applications under development require unusually intensive levels of resources, it may be possible to stay within the thresholds of use offered without cost.

In this chapter, we've worked through a number of considerations that highlight the advantages and disadvantages of cloud computing. Look for advantages and synergies where the technology lines up well with your library's resources and strategies. It might be a good approach to do more with technology in the absence of abundant resources in computer infrastructure and technical personnel. From a cost perspective cloud computing gains an advantage for organizations with more of an ability to support recurring fees that may not have spare funds for large-scale equipment procurements. From a security perspective, cloud computing will be delivered through industrial-strength data centers that follow rigorous practices that stand above the capacity of most library IT departments. Libraries involved with highly sensitive information may gravitate toward private rather than public cloud offerings. Cloud computing delivers high standards of reliability, again exceeding what can be accomplished on local equipment. Yet, cloud-based deployments must also plan for failures, with appropriate disaster recovery, backup procedures, and fail-over contingencies. Environmentally, cloud computing is associated with more efficient use of computing resources, reducing a library's energy use and, extrapolated on a wider scale, a broad decrease in energy consumption. Another benefit lies in the flexibility for library developers to quickly gain access to the resources they need or to work easily in decentralized teams. The downside of cloud computing lies in less local control of computing resources and increased reliance on the

Internet for access to critical systems. Libraries should be aware of all of these trade-offs as they consider incorporating cloud computing into their technology strategies.

▶ 3

PLANNING

- ▶ **Rebalance Budgets for Technology**
- ▶ **Consider Costs**
- ▶ **Negotiate Service-Level Agreements**
- ▶ **Recognize Cloud Computing's Implications for Internet Bandwidth**
- ▶ **Shift to Library Automation in the Cloud**
- ▶ **Consider Application Service Provider Offerings**
- ▶ **Consider Multitenant Software-as-a-Service**
- ▶ **Repositories Move to the Cloud Technologies**
- ▶ **OCLC Embraces the Cloud**
- ▶ **Determine the Cost of Library Automation in the Cloud**

Technology should be a component of the operational and budgetary planning that a library executes in support of its strategic mission. Careful thought should be given to its computing and network infrastructure, the business applications that support its operations, and the technologies involved in the delivery of services to its end users. Cloud computing adds an additional option to the palette of available technologies for the library as it formulates its strategic environment. No technology should be implemented solely because it is new and trendy, but based on a solid business case. A technology such as cloud computing should be adopted when it can be demonstrated that it offers the best functionality and value with the least risk. In this chapter we will look at issues that libraries should consider in their planning process that come into play with cloud computing.

Libraries need to plan for the changes associated with this major shift in technology away from components installed locally toward those delivered through some type of cloud-based service. The degree of impact will vary according to how quickly the library navigates this shift and whether the applications involved provide critical operational support or relate to more incidental types of activities. Switching to an ILS delivered through SaaS requires much more planning than deciding to make use of free cloud services such as Dropbox or Google Apps.

An Inevitable Future?

It should be emphasized that the movement toward delivery of technology through cloud computing is, at least to a certain extent, inevitable. Two decades ago, we saw mainframe computers fall out of favor and eventually become obsolete. The time came when the costs associated with maintaining this model of computing could no longer be sustained as less expensive and more efficient alternatives emerged. In the same way, cloud computing seems to be positioned to grow into increasing level of dominance. In the realm of library systems, many of the newer products are offered only through SaaS.

Even if the library does not have short-term projects under consideration to implement new systems where cloud computing might be an option, long-term planning should take this technology trend into consideration. Over the next decade, most libraries can expect their technology budgets to drift toward subscription-based services and away from local infrastructure.

▶ REBALANCE BUDGETS FOR TECHNOLOGY

The transition to cloud computing has major implications in the way that libraries plan and execute their budgets and allocate resources. Most libraries fund technology projects through a combination of regular budget allocations and up-front costs paid through capital budgets. Local computing infrastructure generally requires significant up-front investments. Initial costs would include the purchase of hardware components such as high-performance servers, redundant disk storage, uninterruptible power sources, tape drives and media for data backup, as well as licenses for the application and supporting components such as operating systems, database management systems, reporting engines, and security products. In addition to these up-front costs, ongoing service and support fees would be part of the annual operating budget. As a broad rule of thumb, the annual maintenance payments are generally around 15 percent of the initial license fee. Every five years or so, the library will need to plan additional capital costs for server replacement and operating system upgrades.

The implementation of similar applications through SaaS assumes a different, much simpler budget model. Instead of the combination of up-front capital expenditures, periodic hardware replacement costs, and annual maintenance fees, the library will need to plan for a single, all-inclusive annual subscription fee. Libraries can expect that the subscription fee associated with SaaS will be higher than the maintenance fee paid for locally hosted applications. This subscription fee covers access to the software, hosting, and support.

As some or all of its computing infrastructure moves to cloud models, the library's budget planning will need to take into consideration the need for higher subscription fees paid annually, which will be offset by savings in periodic purchases of hardware. Less local hardware may also translate into savings in personnel, as noted earlier.

▶ CONSIDER COSTS

Local computing requires the purchase of computing equipment that brings with it a set of expenses, including the purchase of the equipment itself, personnel to maintain it, facilities to house and cool it, service plan fees, and eventually replacement costs. As a general approach, cloud computing trades all of those cost components for monthly subscription fees, either fixed or variable according to consumption. Whether the cost model associated with cloud computing counts as an advantage or disadvantage for the library depends on two factors, local budget preferences and value. From a budget management perspective, the issue hinges on whether funding models favor constant payouts at a moderate level versus higher start-up costs with lower ongoing direct expenses. Stated another way, would a monthly subscription fee for SaaS be easier to accommodate than the start-up costs associated with purchasing a server and software licenses but paying a lower monthly amount for maintenance annually? Some libraries find it easier to obtain one-time funding for projects but have low operating budgets. Grant funding might be available to cover the purchase of equipment but not for longer-term operational costs. For others, the opportunities for one-time project funding may be limited while operational budgets can accommodate reasonable operational expenses.

It's also essential to understand whether local computing or cloud-based alternatives offer the best value in terms of a long-term total cost of ownership analysis. Calculated over a period representing the full life span of the project, how will all the direct and indirect costs associated with local infrastructure compare with the total subscription fees paid for cloud-based services? If one approach offers a higher total cost of ownership than the other, then the library must then carefully decide whether any functional advantages might outweigh the financial issues. Increased local control, for example, might be a result that a library might be willing to pay extra to achieve if the financial analysis came out in favor of SaaS. Strategic repositioning of library technology staff could justify somewhat higher costs of moving to cloud-based deployment of routine infrastructure components. So, while libraries may not always choose the cheapest alternative, they must seek the best value.

▶ NEGOTIATE SERVICE-LEVEL AGREEMENTS

Any time that an organization subscribes to a set of cloud-based services as part of its critical infrastructure, it should pay careful attention to the terms of the subscription contract that specify exactly what guarantees come with the services provided. A contract for computing resources through a cloud provider will naturally specify what resources will be provided to the customer and what fees the customer will pay. These contracts should also include service-level agreements that specify the allowable percentages of downtime, response times for service issues, the performance of transactions, and other metrics that quantify acceptable delivery of the computing resources and what remedies the provider will implement should the service levels fall below the stated requirements.

It's also important to keep in mind that major problems can take place without triggering service-level agreements. When an organization contracts for raw computing resources through IaaS, it continues to be responsible for the proper functioning of its software applications and data integrity. If a library operates its ILS in a cloud infrastructure such as Amazon's EC2 service, and it experiences a software malfunction that results in corrupt data and downtime of its catalog, it's unlikely that Amazon would bear any actionable responsibility. Operating applications in a cloud environment does not mitigate the need to implement adequate contingency planning for data backup and restoration procedures.

In addition to negotiating the best service-level agreement, the library will need to plan any necessary contingencies beyond its terms. Even if the agreement specifies that the provider will perform and maintain backup copies of data, the library may want to also implement replicates of the data outside the service provider. The library may choose to regularly copy data to media it holds locally or to another storage service provider. These measures can mitigate risk in the event of a technical error, business failure, or other events that might cause a disruption in the service.

▶ RECOGNIZE CLOUD COMPUTING'S IMPLICATIONS FOR INTERNET BANDWIDTH

Cloud computing makes a major impact on an organization's use of Internet bandwidth. It will increase the organization's dependence on its Internet connectivity and will result in increases in the bandwidth used. The pathways of access differ fundamentally when deployed through a cloud-based service compared to local infrastructure. The traffic between end users and the service flows through the provider's Internet connections instead of the library's more limited connection. Likewise, library personnel will connect to the service via the Internet rather than through the library's local network. Assuming that the traffic involved to support end users exceeds that for in-library use, the provision of services through cloud-based services should decrease the organization's overall bandwidth consumption. Especially for high-volume web-based services, a remotely hosted deployment may save the organization considerable expense in its telecommunication costs associated with upgrading Internet bandwidth.

A service based on cloud infrastructure in most cases should also result in much higher performance and reliability than would be possible through an organization's local Internet connection. Providers of cloud-based services maintain very high bandwidth connections to the Internet, typically through multiple providers. Most large-scale data centers associated with cloud service providers have sufficient redundant connectivity that even if their primary Internet connection suffers a disruption, access continues through alternate pathways.

These differences in the patterns of Internet bandwidth should be considered when planning for technology infrastructure and corresponding budgets. A library needs to constantly monitor its incoming and outgoing bandwidth and at least on an annual basis make adjustments with its Internet service provider to ensure that it has adequate capacity to meet demand.

Even when its core services are provided externally through cloud-based services, the library's connectivity to the Internet continues to serve a critical role. This connection connects all in-library computers to the Internet, including workstations provided for library patrons and computers used by library personnel, as well as wireless networks provided for public access. A library's Internet connection needs to be sized not only to support connectivity to any applications that it may have deployed through external service providers, but it also must provide access to an increasing number of remote electronic resources. As more of these resources come in the form of multimedia audio and video, bandwidth demands may increase considerably.

▶ SHIFT TO LIBRARY AUTOMATION IN THE CLOUD

Libraries make major investments in the core automation systems that help them manage their operations and provide access to their collections and services. The ILS, also called the library management system in regions outside the United States, delivers automation support for the operations of the library, especially in the areas of acquiring, cataloging, and circulating collection materials, and offers access and self-service features to library users through its built-in online catalog. Discovery products provide access to a wider view of library collections, going beyond the materials managed directly within the ILS to include other digital collections and the resources available through the library's subscriptions to electronic content products. Given the strategic importance and the financial investments that libraries make in their core automation and discovery platforms, it's essential that they operate in the most efficient ways and make use of the most appropriate technologies. It's essential to explore and take advantage of the most efficient and appropriate technology models. These issues of choosing the best technology architectures and deployment models apply to each of the major components in a library's strategic technology environment, including ILSs, discovery interfaces, institutional repositories, asset management systems, and digital preservation platforms.

A shift from locally implemented automation systems to alternatives that deliver equivalent functionality through cloud-based services can make a dramatic impact on the way that a library manages its technology resources. Reliance on SaaS instead of operating local equipment reorients personnel away from dealing with servers, operating systems, and other infrastructure issues toward more concentration on higher-level functional and strategic activities.

While the implementation of cloud computing makes a major difference to organizations or departments involved in providing and supporting technology, it will largely be transparent to the organizations and individuals that make use of the resulting products. The shift to cloud computing might completely redefine the part of a library organization responsible for the management of its automation systems. The administrative unit of a consortium or of a public or university library system, for example, might operate an ILS and other application on behalf of a set of branches and facilities that comprise the organization. Moving to SaaS is tantamount to outsourcing significant portions of the support structures.

Libraries that share computing resources managed by a consortium, branches of a public library system, divisional libraries, or others that use but don't manage an automation system should experience little change. The way that these libraries make use of the system will change very little depending on whether the system is managed by their central administrative unit or through a vendor-hosted SaaS arrangement.

▶ CONSIDER APPLICATION SERVICE PROVIDER OFFERINGS

As we noted in Chapter 2, one of the popular arrangements for traditional library automation applications involves a deployment model where the vendor provides all hosting and management of the software. The customer library accesses the system through the Internet, using the same client software as would be used with a local installation, which might be a graphical user interface running under Windows, Mac, or Linux, a Java-based graphical client, or a purely web-based interface. In this flavor of SaaS, the provider will operate a separate instance of the software for each library system or consortium, which distinguishes it from multitenant SaaS where many unrelated organizations participate in a shared instance. This allows a library to gain benefits such as relief from local hosting, hardware and operating support, and subscription pricing while using well-established automation products.

Libraries involved with a traditional ILS that they have implemented locally will eventually find the need to upgrade or replace the server hardware. Many libraries may find the approaching demise of older server hardware as an opportunity to reassess whether they should relinquish their self-hosting arrangement and shift to an application service provider arrangement. Almost all of the major ILSs vendors offer hosted versions of their products and often will give significant incentives to adopt this approach rather than local installations. The delivery of ILSs through application service provider arrangements, in recent years positioned as a version of SaaS, has been a routine alternative for over a decade, with an ever-increasing number of libraries choosing this approach.

SirsiDynix, one of the largest library automation vendors globally, emphasizes SaaS as one of its strategic deployment options. The company markets its major automation and discovery products through SaaS, including the Symphony and Horizon library management systems, the Enterprise discovery platform, and the recently launched Portfolio digital asset management system. As of early 2011 SirsiDynix reports that over 700 of its customer libraries deploy either Horizon or Symphony through the SaaS offering. The number of libraries moving to the company's SaaS includes those moving from local installations of the same product as well as those implementing the system for the first time. The initial versions of the Enterprise discovery interface were available only through SaaS; only in more recent versions can libraries install the software locally. Portfolio's orientation toward SaaS as the primary development and deployment model reflects this company's strategy as the prevailing industry trend.

At least three of the predecessor companies that now constitute SirsiDynix became involved in this type of arrangement in 2000, when Sirsi Corporation began offering its Unicorn ILS through Sirsi.net, which was also the year that epixtech, Inc. (later Dynix Corporation) became an application service provider for the Horizon ILS; Data Research Associates began its application service provider product in 2000. Ex Libris has offered Aleph, MetaLib, and

SFX in application service provider configurations since 2000; this company launched VoyagerPlus in early 2011, a fully hosted and managed service based on the Voyager ILS, and offers Primo Total Care, a hosted version of its core discovery platform. VTLS has offered its Virtua ILS through application service provider since 2003.

Innovative Interfaces may have been the first to offer an application service provider deployment of an ILS when it launched its INN-Keeper service in April 1997 with the Western State University College of Law and the Thomas Jefferson School of Law as early adopters.

Civica Library and Learning is an international company that offers the Spydus library management system in both locally installed and hosted versions. Outside the United States, the application service provider model is usually called "managed services." Over half of the libraries using the Spydus library management system have implemented the managed service option.

Similar hosting arrangements are also available for open source library automation systems. Most libraries that implement an open source library automation system, such as Koha or Evergreen, rely on conversion, installation, and support services from a commercial provider. A large portion of these installations also rely on the support firm to provide hosting services, resulting in an implementation quite similar to the application service provider offerings seen with the proprietary systems. Koha and Evergreen both incorporate designs that lend themselves to individual instances of the application established for each library system or consortium that adopts the system rather than shared instances.

Some of the vender-hosted installations of open source automation systems make use of IaaS. LibLime, for example, deploys its LibLime Academic Koha using Amazon EC2, providing a high performance environment for its clients. LibLime reports that it deploys over 90 percent of its installations through this model of SaaS.

► CONSIDER MULTITENANT SOFTWARE-AS-A-SERVICE

Library automation applications designed and developed in more recent years incorporate more current technology architectures, including adherence to the service-oriented architecture, more reliance on web-based interfaces instead of graphical clients, and orientation toward multitenant SaaS. Library automation applications designed under the client/server architecture targeting one installation per library, library system, or consortium implementing the system cannot easily be transformed into more pure deployments of SaaS where a single instance is designed to serve multiple independent organizations making use of the software. These traditional applications can gain many of the benefits of SaaS through vender-hosted application service provider arrangements, but they fall short of delivering the full menu of benefits the more modern approach affords. In this section we will review some of the library automation products that embrace the more modern understanding of SaaS that goes beyond vendor hosting of traditional software.

Serials Solutions (http://www.serialssolutions.com/) has recently announced its Intota library services platform and currently offers products related to the management of and access to electronic resources, including 360 Core, the entry product for management and access of a library's electronic resources; 360 Resource Manager, a full-featured electronic resource management system; 360 Link, providing linking to article content through OpenURL link resolution; 360 Access Control, a service for patron authentication and access, and 360 Search, a federated search engine. These products rely on KnowledgeWorks, a centralized repository of data that details the specific titles and date coverage of each of the packages represented in the body of content products that potentially comprise a library's subscriptions. Serials Solutions launched its Summon discovery service in 2009 based on a consolidated index of article-level content that is deployed through SaaS. These products are not available for local installation, a key indicator of a true software-as-a-service design, and make use of shared comprehensive data components, profiled according to the holdings of each library implementing the service.

Ex Libris (http://www.exlibrisgroup.com/), though most of its current products were designed for traditional deployment, has embraced cloud technologies for its newly developed offerings. Its Aleph and Voyager ILSs target academic and research libraries, most of which install the software on local computing infrastructure. Ex Libris has offered Voyager only since early 2011 through a fully managed hosted service. The company's discovery product Primo, launched in 2006, was designed for individual local installations, though since 2010 it has offered a hosted version branded as Primo TotalCare.

In 2009 Ex Libris created a consolidate index of article-level content, named Primo Central, to expand the capabilities of the core Primo discovery interface. Primo Central, though not a separate software product, is deployed using cloud-based technologies in an instance of Primo shared by all libraries that subscribe to the service. Ex Libris has implemented Primo Central through Amazon EC2 and S3 IaaS.

Alma (http://www.exlibrisgroup.com/category/AlmaOverview), Ex Libris's next-generation library automation platform, fully embraces cloud computing. Scheduled for general release in early 2012, Alma will be deployed as a multi-tenant SaaS using all web-based clients and will be deployed using IaaS. The data model of Alma includes broadly shared resources, called the Community Zone, accessible by all libraries that participate in the service. It also includes the ability to support partitions of data specific to each library, called the Library Zone, for inventory and collections specific to the organization implementing the product. While Alma has been designed as for multi-tenant SaaS, Ex Libris will also support instances of the software for local installation, either on local hardware or cloud-based infrastructure. LIBIS, a large consortium in Belgium, for example, will implement Alma using this approach to support its member libraries in a way that localizes shared data within the consortium's service area.

Biblionix (http://www.biblionix.com/), a Texas-based company, provides a library automation product called Apollo to small public libraries through SaaS. Biblionix explains that Apollo was designed as a true multitenant SaaS application, with each instance capable of supporting all the libraries that use the product. It operates multiple instances, however, for the purpose of load balancing and to provide redundancy to increase the reliability of the services. Biblionix reports it benefits from having all its customers run the same version of the service, with new versions and features deployed simultaneously. Another added advantage involves the ability to simplify interactions with external vendors, such as for connections to interlibrary loan systems. Apollo provides an example of how SaaS can be leveraged to produce a web-based library automation system for small public libraries at an affordable cost.

The Kuali OLE project (http://kuali.org/ole) is underway to create an open source, enterprise-oriented library automation environment for academic and research libraries, with partial funding through a grant from the Andrew W. Mellon Foundation. Though the finished product will be initially deployed on local infrastructure at each of the organizations in the partnership, the project makes extensive use of cloud technologies, exemplifying the advantages of this technology for software development. The Kuali OLE project engaged HTC Global Services, a software development firm with off-shore programmers in India, to perform software design, coding, and quality assurance tasks. The use of Amazon's cloud-based infrastructure provides support for this globally distributed software development endeavor. Programming takes place in India using Agile methodologies that produce code quickly for small components of the system in rapid succession. The development partner libraries test each iteration of new functionality from locations throughout the United States. The project has been a proving ground for the ability for cloud technologies to provide a flexible development environment. Project participants indicate that the use of this shared cloud-based infrastructure has been much more efficient than would be the case if the changes had to be installed on servers for each institution involved with the project.

In recent years, additional components complement the ILS, such as discovery products and services. With a broader scope than the content managed within the ILS and with more modern features, discovery systems have supplanted the online catalog modules for an increasing number of libraries. While some discovery services may function as next-generation library catalogs, offering a more modern interface to basically the same content as the integrated library system, many—especially those oriented to academic libraries—offer comprehensive indexes that span the library's traditional print collection, plus individual articles represented in subscriptions to electronic content products, institutional repositories, and collections of digital materials. As with the ILS, the deployment options of discovery products include local installations, with a growing trend toward SaaS offerings.

BiblioCommons (http://www.bibliocommons.com/), a new-generation catalog interface for public libraries based on social networking concepts, is delivered through a multitenant SaaS platform. BiblioCommons was developed by a company of the same name based in Toronto, Ontario, Canada. The product was initially implemented primarily by libraries in Canada, such as the Oakville Public Library, which served as the pilot site beginning in July 2009, and by the Edmonton Public Library and others in the provinces of Alberta, British Columbia, and Ontario. BiblioCommons has also been implemented in libraries throughout the United States, and New Zealand. Other major municipal libraries in North America implementing BiblioCommons include New York Public Library, Seattle Public Library, Boston Public Library, the Ottawa Public Library, Vancouver Public Library, the CLEVNET consortium in Ohio, and the Whatcom County Library System in Washington. It has been implemented by the Christchurch City Libraries in New Zealand and the Yarra Plenty Regional Library in Australia. A single instance of the BiblioCommons platform serves all the libraries subscribing to the service. BiblioCommons includes a suite of application programming interfaces (APIs) that allow libraries to develop their own applications against the platform and to connect with external systems. Each library that subscribes to BiblioCommons makes use of customized indexes derived from their local collections, with connections into the ILS that dynamically present the status and location of any item viewed and to present patron services such as hold requests and renewals.

BiblioCommons embraces all the characteristics of true SaaS, including multiple organizations sharing a single instance, but with the ability to implement local branding, configuration, customizations, and delivery of the application through a web-based interface.

Access to APIs

In addition to the web-based or graphical interfaces provided with an ILS, many libraries take advantage of APIs to support connections to other business systems or to accommodate local programming to accomplish ad hoc reporting or other extensions of functionality.

When considering an ILS through an SaaS deployment, libraries that expect access to APIs need to determine the extent to which they are available. There may be differences between the levels of access to APIs offered on vendor-hosted systems relative to what is possible with local installations. Libraries that intend to use a third-party discovery interface, for example, will need to be sure that all the data synchronization capabilities and APIs required will be available.

▶ REPOSITORIES MOVE TO THE CLOUD TECHNOLOGIES

Libraries can also implement institutional repository functions, digital collections, and digital preservation activities through cloud technologies. Two of the primary open source platforms for institutional repositories, DSpace and the Fedora Commons, merged into a common governance organization called "DuraSpace" (http://www.duraspace.org/). In addition to ongoing development and maintenance, the DuraSpace organization will create a new product based on both technologies called "DuraCloud" (http://duracloud.org/). As implied by its name, it will employ cloud technologies to deliver a flexible service for storage, long-term digital preservation, and access to objects in a digital repository. The levels of protection required to support rigorous standards of preservation are accomplished by storing each object through multiple cloud storage service providers, including Amazon S3, Rackspace CloudFiles, and EMC Atmos. The DuraCloud service includes a DuraStore web application that provides an interface into the storage services that manage the digital objects, including the distribution and validation of copies across the multiple cloud storage services. Another set of services supports access to the digital objects through the creation of derivative images, streaming video, and other tasks related to accessing and viewing the objects. DuraSpace has been in a pilot stage since 2009, but they announced the launch of DuraCloud as a production service in November 2011.

▶ OCLC EMBRACES THE CLOUD

Of all the organizations providing technology and data services to libraries, OCLC has some of the strongest associations with cloud computing. OCLC's mantra asserts that libraries will increase their impact as they move from isolated individual systems to a globally shared infrastructure and stands in a unique position to deliver this capacity to libraries, building on the organization's mission, worldwide presence, and massive data resources. The organization's core bibliographic database, WorldCat, stands as the world's largest repository of library metadata and is the basis of cataloging services for OCLC's member libraries throughout the world. OCLC has steadily expanded the services surrounding WorldCat to include resource sharing and interlibrary loan. WorldCat Local was launched as a discovery service in 2007. In 2009, OCLC announced its ambitious agenda to take WorldCat to yet another level of functionality to include circulation, acquisitions, license management, and other features that would allow it to function as a library's comprehensive automation environment. This new product, now known as "WorldShare Management Services," would eliminate the need for a library to operate a local ILS. WorldShare Management Services would involve the creation of a new technology infrastructure that theoretically would be capable of handling the transactions of all the libraries in the world and would leverage the World-Cat database of bibliographic records to support item-level transactions. Libraries opting to implement OCLC's WorldShare Management Services use web-based clients to perform tasks otherwise associated with ILS modules such as circulation, cataloging, and acquisitions. The data models involved contrast with traditional automation products in that all libraries share bibliographic records in WorldCat, attaching holdings and items as needed. The concept of importing or transferring bibliographic records into a local system no longer applies, because no local system needs to exist with this approach.

WorldShare Management Services fits into several aspects of the cloud-based computing models. Deployed as multitenant SaaS, it eliminates the need for a library to operate its own local automation system. It is operated entirely through web-based clients, including both staff and end-user access. All organizations that make use of the service participate in a single shared instance. The data related to the operation of WorldShare Management Services resides entirely within OCLC's infrastructure.

OCLC operates WorldShare Management Services on computing infrastructure it owns and maintains rather than on IaaS provided through a third party. OCLC has a long history of maintaining large-scale computing services and has created redundant, geographically distributed fail-over facilities should problems arise with its primary data center housed at its headquarters in Dublin, Ohio.

One of the key characteristics of WorldShare Management Services relates to the data services provided. In addition to the well-known WorldCat bibliographic database, the product will make use of many other shared repositories of data, providing much greater efficiencies than alternatives in which each library maintains its own local files. Examples include a shared repository of vendors from which libraries acquire materials. Through the use of a shared vendor registry, libraries can tag onto an existing vendor record for their orders, adding any library-specific elements when needed. The general data structure of WorldShare Management Services allows libraries to make use of globally shared records, with the ability to add local information and with granular controls in place to restrict the libraries using the system from viewing or altering another library's local information. Other examples of shared data structures within WorldShare Management Services include the WorldCat knowledge base that includes data on e-content products in support of electronic resource management and in the discovery and linking needed for end-user services. WorldShare Management Services provides support for the internal operations of a library. While WorldCat Local most easily integrates with it as the library's discovery interface, other third-party products could be used as well.

In addition to the basic functionality that OCLC will deliver through WorldShare Management Services, it also anticipates that libraries will want to create additional tools and services to fulfill local needs. OCLC offers a set of APIs that allow libraries to tap into data and functionality resources through the WorldShare Platform. Through this set of APIs, OCLC delivers a platform to support third-party applications that might be created by libraries, vendors, or other organizations. OCLC facilitates a developer's network by providing a collaborative environment to foster development activities.

WorldShare Management Services presses cloud-based library automation to its logical conclusion. The product, in development since about 2008, entered the early adoption cycle in 2010, with over 20 libraries using the product as their production automation environment by mid-2011.

▶ DETERMINE THE COST OF LIBRARY AUTOMATION IN THE CLOUD

One of the fundamental realities of budget planning for large technology projects involves the absence of published price lists for software and related services. Vendors scale prices according to the size and complexity of the organization and to the specific modules and options selected. Although some rough formula may be used to calculate a base price, the final offer may also include factors relative to specific competitive bidding scenarios. Prices may also change in the process of contract negotiations. Some of the factors that come into play in the pricing for major business application such as an ILS include:

> ▶ The population served by the organization implementing the application. For academic libraries the relevant metric might include the full-time enrollment of the college or university; for public libraries the number of registered patrons would apply.

▶ The number of personnel operating the software, which may be expressed as the number of copies licensed for the staff client software. Variables to consider include whether this is the total number of potential users of the software or the maximum number of simultaneous users.

▶ The size of the collections managed, including the number of metadata records and total items or objects.

▶ Modules or options selected. For an ILS, the library will select which of the major modules it requires, such as cataloging, circulation, serials management, acquisitions, or online catalog. Other components that may involve additional cost include system-to-system interfaces such as enabling the SIP2 (system interchange protocol, version 2) protocol for self-service stations, NCIP (NISO Circulation Interchange Protocol) for interlibrary loan or resource sharing, Z39.50 client to search and download bibliographic records from external sources, and Z39.50 server to enable search of the system by external applications. Access to the full set of APIs may involve an additional fee to enable access as well as costs for mandatory training programs. Application software vendors may reasonably expect that organizations that use the APIs go through certification or training courses, because their improper use can result in data corruption problems that their customer support departments would need to rectify.

Budget Model for Software-as-a-Service

A pure SaaS environment can offer a budget model as simple as a set monthly or annual subscription fee. While this subscription fee may be higher than what a library might be accustomed to pay for the maintenance of locally installed applications, it's important to keep in mind the offsetting costs.

Even in an SaaS arrangement, there may be some other costs that need to be included in budget planning. In the migration from an existing ILS to a new one delivered through SaaS, there may be transition costs. Depending on the circumstances, exit fees may apply to the incumbent system for data extraction or other services that may be needed as the organization terminates its use.

As seen in this chapter, cloud-based options permeate the products and services related to library automation and resource discovery. Established products that predate current expectations for SaaS can be deployed through vender-hosted arrangements that deliver similar benefits. The movement toward cloud computing goes beyond the core management system; applications across all the different areas that support library operations, collection management, and patron interfaces are increasingly offered through options other than the traditional approach of installation on local servers. This chapter included numerous examples, across several product categories, but should not be considered an exhaustive survey.

The trend toward cloud-based library automation also should not be taken in a way that devalues the incumbent model that relies on software installed on local servers. For many libraries, the local computing model will continue to work quite well for many years to come. Those that require a high degree of local control, have sufficient personnel for managing technical infrastructure, that require highly customized applications, or that have jurisdictional or policy requirements that restrict the way that they store institutional data may not be in a position to take advantage of key automation systems deployed through cloud technologies. Over the next decade, however, if current trends prevail, the number of products offered primarily through SaaS will increase as will the proportions of libraries opting for this approach.

▶4

SOCIAL MECHANICS

- ▶ **Develop Service and Support for Technology**
- ▶ **Reshape Personnel Support for Technology**
- ▶ **Attend to Policy and Privacy Issues**
- ▶ **Coordinate with Institutional Information Technology**
- ▶ **Maintain a View from the Top**

Shifting from a model of local computing to one where an increasing amount of the technical infrastructure is based on externally provided cloud-based services can potentially alter much of the organizational processes that relate to technology. Processes with potential impact include budget, technology support both within the library and with central IT departments, and staff training.

▶DEVELOP SERVICE AND SUPPORT FOR TECHNOLOGY

As a library makes increased use of cloud computing services, it needs to reassess its structures for service and support of technology. In a model where the library relies on local computing infrastructure, it is essential to have technology personnel on hand who are responsible for its operation and maintenance. How many and what type of personnel involved would be proportional to the quantity and complexity of the applications the library has to support. The procedures, and their documentation, will need to be adjusted to clarify what service tasks continue to be directed to local library personnel and which need to be directed to an external provider. Yet, the use of cloud-based applications does not mean that in all cases library staff would contact the provider directly. For major applications such as the ILS, routine problems and requests would continue to be directed to the designated manager of that system in the library, who would then either satisfy the request if possible or open a service call with the provider. For most operational issues, whether the application is provided through SaaS or operates on local computers should be largely transparent. The differences lie more in the impact it makes on the personnel who deal directly with technology.

As an organization shifts portions of its computing infrastructure to cloud-based services, its burden for providing technical support and services to its general population should generally diminish. Lightening the load for such support services ranks as one of the key goals gained in moving to this approach. Deployment of SaaS and IaaS removes many layers of technology that would otherwise require considerable in-house support.

That said, responsibilities for support do not vanish entirely. Regardless of how an organization deploys the applications involved in its operations or in how it serves its constituents, it must have processes in place to deliver high-quality services. By not having to allocate as many resources to lower-level infrastructure issues, the organization can focus more on the higher-level issues that have a more direct impact on its users.

For libraries, moving to cloud computing for its core automation or discovery services enables an upward shift in the focus of its services. One of the most appealing characteristics involves allowing libraries to spend less time with routine technical maintenance and pay more attention to the needs of patrons. Again, less time devoted to deep technical tasks such as server and operating system maintenance translates into more resources that can be channeled into other activities.

To the extent that cloud-based automation systems live up to their potential for increased reliability, the library should spend less time dealing with system failures. It would be unrealistic to assume that issues would never arise. Especially consider that problems with the library's connectivity to the Internet will remain as the most critical vulnerability. When problems occur, designated personnel in the library become the intermediaries who work with the vendor to resolve the failure.

With the onus of service and support more on the shoulders of the venders supplying the software application to the library, their quality and responsiveness become critical for the library. Clear procedures and lines of communication need to be in place so that any problems experienced can be reported promptly to the vendor. Depending on the service arrangement, requests and problems may need to be submitted through a specific individual or department in the library.

▶ RESHAPE PERSONNEL SUPPORT FOR TECHNOLOGY

The approach that a library chooses in the way it deploys its automation applications is a major consideration in how it shapes its staffing capacity for technology. Organizations that rely mostly on cloud computing will see different patterns for the numbers and types of technology positions than those that depend on locally installed systems. Operating local installations of its major business applications requires some personnel to be allocated in several different roles. In larger libraries with multiple systems in place, these roles may be represented in specialists in discrete positions. In others, multiple roles can be taken on by a single person with more general expertise. Some of the key roles involved in library technology support include the following:

▶ The systems administrator manages the server hardware and operating system. Routine tasks would include keeping the operating system current with system updates and security patches, implementing data backup and disaster recovery procedures, system tuning to ensure optimal performance, and monitoring the allocation of disk storage.

▶ The network administrator manages the organization's internal network. Activities would include maintaining the general health of the organization's network and diagnosing and correcting connectivity problems. This role might also include installing, configuring, and maintaining network components such as Ethernet switches, routers, and firewalls. In regard to the applications such as the library's ILS, activities would include ensuring connectivity between the server and staff clients and managing bandwidth to end users on the organization's network and through the Internet. In some cases, the use of VPN (virtual private network) components may be necessary to ensure the security and privacy of data held within the application, especially for those using staff clients remotely from the Internet or on unsecured wireless networks.

▶ The database administrator (DBA) takes responsibility for the optimal performance of the database platform used by one or more business applications. Any major relational database requires detailed knowledge of general practices and procedures that apply across all products as well as its own variants. Especially for complex systems a DBA plays an important role in ensuring the proper tuning of the database environment to ensure fast performance for both online transactions and batch operations such as data loads as well as safeguarding the system to prevent and recovering from any corruption of data.

▶ If the organization expects to extend the application through the use of APIs or to perform customization beyond the standard configuration options, then it may make use of an application programmer who can create scripts or utility software to accomplish these tasks. The programmer would need to have detailed knowledge of any available

APIs and data structures involved, as well as an understanding of the general architecture and functionality of the application in addition to fluency in the programming languages supported.

▶ Computer technicians provide assistance for the computer workstations, printers, and other peripherals used by personnel in the library and those provided for patrons. These technicians would respond to problems as they arise, apply software updates, install new equipment or software, and perform other technical tasks.

▶ The website manager takes responsibility for the technical administration of the library's website and may have a coordinating role in its design and content. The scale of this role varies according to the size and complexity of the library. For very large libraries, this person would likely work with a content management system such as Drupal, Joomla, or Microsoft SharePoint or may use Adobe Dreamweaver or other web publishing software. Any of the standard techniques for creating a library's website can be accomplished on either a locally housed server or a site hosted through a cloud service.

▶ A systems librarian, in the context of an ILS, takes responsibility for configuring and managing the product to meet the needs of the library. Tasks might include developing and implementing system configuration details such as circulation rule policy tables, configuring indexing and display options relative to MARC tags, scheduling circulation notices, and a wide range of other activities.

Shifting from a traditional locally installed library automation system to one delivered through SaaS will eliminate, or at least reduce, the personnel roles that the library will need to support locally.

The specific types of personnel impacted by the adoption of cloud computing will differ according to the types of services implemented, but some general observations apply. Moving core applications from local installations to SaaS lessens the need for personnel in the roles of systems administration, database administration, and applications programming. Most or all of the technical activities dealing with managing hardware and operating systems that underlie the application are handled by the vendor.

Adopting cloud-based applications does not, however, eliminate the need for the organization to maintain its local network. If anything, the requirements for the local network will become more critical as the organization makes increased use of external services. Satisfactory performance of cloud computing depends on a well-managed local network, fault-tolerant pathways to the Internet, and ample bandwidth. Organizations that deal with sensitive or confidential data will need to pay close attention to the security of their network and will need to implement end-to-end encryption transmissions, such as are provided through VPN technologies.

The extent to which a library will need a dedicated systems librarian when the core automation system is delivered through SaaS will also vary. While many of the internals of the system will be managed by the vendor, the library may continue to need to support higher-level tasks related to the configuration and operation of applications such as maintaining circulation policy tables, running standard and customized reports, branding and customizing end-user interfaces, or other standard activities that a systems librarian would perform on a locally installed automation system. Some arrangements, on the other hand, involve all such changes being implemented by the vendor without intervention by library staff. How these tasks are divided between the vendor and the librarian will need to be well understood in advance, and how they are stipulated will influence the library's need to support a systems librarian and how that position's effort is allocated.

Cloud computing can be implemented by libraries with more complex requirements that involve custom functionality of their system or that need to make connections with other infrastructure components. These libraries will need technical personnel capable of performing the necessary systems integration tasks.

Applications deployed through SaaS have the same capability to offer APIs that allow library programmers to gain access to the data and functionality contained within the system through their own scripts or software programs. These programming techniques can also be used to establish dynamic connections with other components of the organization's technical infrastructure such as authentication services, enterprise resource planning systems, or learning management systems. Whether an application is installed locally or through an SaaS subscription does not impose technical restrictions on whether it is possible to use APIs. The key factors include whether the system has been created in ways that expose APIs and the policies, documentation, and procedures under which access to APIs are provided by the vendor.

Libraries with an interest in taking advantage of the APIs of their automation systems will stipulate this requirement as part of their selection and procurement process. An important question to raise is whether the vendor provides the same level of access to APIs for a hosted system as they do when the system is installed on the library's local infrastructure. It would be problematic, for example, if the library relied on certain APIs of their ILS for the support of a discovery system, and they lost that capability through a migration to SaaS.

Cloud computing does not necessarily preclude the need for programmers in the library. Whether or not the library needs to have programmers within their organization depends more on their interest or requirements to implement complex interoperability among their applications and those of its parent organization, to develop custom functionality, and to perform advanced data extraction and analysis. If a library is involved in these activities with its locally installed system, it will continue to do so should it shift some or all applications to SaaS. The deployment model in most cases will be neutral relative to these activities and the technical personnel support involved.

These examples show that cloud computing has major implications for library personnel allocations. For some libraries, the need to reduce staffing may drive a move to cloud models such as SaaS. In other cases, cloud computing provides opportunities to redirect the activities of technology-oriented positions away from routine system maintenance and toward more creative projects.

▶ ATTEND TO POLICY AND PRIVACY ISSUES

In addition to technical and organizational considerations, libraries need to attend to policy issues that may come into play with the use of cloud computing. As libraries engage in cloud-based services that involve changes to the way that information might be accessed or shared, careful review should be given to how it complies with institutional privacy policies or applicable governmental regulations. A technical review should confirm whether the cloud service provides adequate network security to protect any sensitive information. Libraries should require that any cloud services meet or exceed the network security delivered on local systems. For libraries involved with student or health information, FERPA and HIPAA regulations may apply to some types of information that they manage. Regardless whether the infrastructure is local or cloud based, libraries dealing with data subject to these regulations will need to audit the procedures, software, and infrastructure involved to ensure compliance.

Some libraries may have jurisdictional concerns. Some countries, for example, may have laws that require that publicly owned or managed data reside within the country. Such restrictions will limit use of public cloud infrastructure if options are not available to abide by such geographic restrictions.

▶ COORDINATE WITH INSTITUTIONAL INFORMATION TECHNOLOGY

Today, computing systems tend to be deployed on an enterprise level rather than having separate departments within the organization implement their own applications. Most large organizations, such as colleges, universities, local governments, and corporations, would run a single e-mail system, accounting system, or content management system. It's standard practice for a library to be required to participate in the e-mail system of its parent organization. Sharing business and communications across the organization facilitates better communication and collaboration. These arrangements also gain efficiencies through centralized administration rather than redundant efforts throughout the organization.

Libraries that operate within an institutional enterprise computing environment will not likely want to unilaterally move to cloud-based applications independently. It might be counterproductive, for example, for a library to move its personnel from an institutional e-mail system to Gmail or to one of its cloud-based counterparts. Such a move might have an isolating effect on the library relative to its parent organization. Such a move should be made only in cases of widespread difficulties with the institutionally provided environment.

Many large organizations, on the other hand, have begun delivering their institutional enterprise applications through cloud-based services. Many universities, for example, have moved to such programs as Google Apps for Education as the basis for their institutional e-mail and productivity environment.

Libraries not closely aligned with a parent organization will have much more flexibility regarding how they manage their business environment. If the library has to maintain its own mail systems, network storage, and productivity applications on its own, then it may see benefits in moving to cloud-based services.

Library-specific applications are less likely to fall under the umbrella of the parent organization. Such products as the ILS, OpenURL link resolver, electronic resource management systems, or digital collections platforms may fall more under the administrative control of the library than its parent organization. Libraries will have flexibility to choose whether such applications will be deployed locally or through cloud services. These systems may have points of connection with enterprise components, such as authentication services or student management systems, which require coordination with the institutional IT department. In most cases, interoperability can be established between library-specific applications and institutional components just as easily when using products deployed through cloud services as when installed locally. These issues should be part of the ongoing technical and administrative coordination that takes place between the library and its parent organization.

▶ MAINTAIN A VIEW FROM THE TOP

Any movement toward a greater adoption of cloud-based computing should be well integrated with the library's broad technology strategies. Consideration of service-based technologies needs to be integrated into the library's strategic planning process, not made through an ad hoc manner. As we have noted elsewhere, the move to cloud computing is not an all-or-nothing proposition, so the degree to which a library shifts away from local infrastructure should be part of a coherent technology strategy. Furthermore, library administrators may not necessarily need to be involved in the technical details, but they do need to be aware of the broad implications for the organization.

Increased reliance on cloud computing infrastructure is tantamount to outsourcing technology services, which, as we have seen, has an impact on many aspects of the library's operations. The deployment of the library's major automation system, for example, through a SaaS or application service provider arrangement may involve less local control, the need for fewer in-house technology personnel, and more reliance on—and vulnerability to—the provider.

To a certain degree, investigation and experimentation with cloud-based services can take place at a grassroots level within the library. Any larger-scale adoption, however, needs to be integrated into the official planning process. Library personnel advocating the use of cloud computing should be sure that any informal use of this approach is consistent with library policies and with its overall technology policies and procedures. It's possible to imagine scenarios, for example, where important library data may be saved on a cloud storage service, outside the protection of the routine backup procedures, leading to increased vulnerability. As with any new technology, it's important to allow for innovation and exploration, yet incorporation of any new approach should be handled strategically.

Well-informed decisions should be made with full awareness of how data will be handled. If the primary version of the data resides within the vendor's infrastructure, will copies be provided regularly to the library? If the vendor withdraws the service, or even goes out of business, will this result in a major disruption for the library, and what contingency plans could be put in place? Will all the data be handled in full compliance with applicable policies and regulations, such as HIPAA and FERPA? For many public or governmental institutions, routine communications handled through e-mail may be subject to open records policies, and procedures may need to be devised for ensuring proper security, disclosure, and archiving. All of these types of questions should be part of the planning process prior to engaging in these services.

There may also be times when a top-down approach to the implementation of cloud computing services to allocate library resources according to key library priorities and strategies is best. Library administrators may conclude that resources should be channeled in other directions rather than toward maintaining local systems. Staff invested in these local systems may resist such strategies especially for major automation systems, because the shift from a local installation to SaaS is a form of outsourcing of technology support. As with other cases of outsourcing, such a strategy may conflict with the preferences of some library personnel. But it's important for a library to deploy its scarce resources strategically, and it may also be the case that the shift to SaaS in one area of the library's infrastructure will enable the library to refocus its technology personnel to other areas where they can help produce more innovative services that have a greater positive impact.

▶5

IMPLEMENTATION

- ▶ Leverage the Cloud for Supplemental Storage
- ▶ Use Google Apps in Your Library
- ▶ Provide Cloud-Based E-mail on a Large Scale
- ▶ Power a Static Library Website from the Cloud Using Amazon S3
- ▶ Power Your Dynamic Library Website from the Cloud Using Amazon EC2
- ▶ Power a Web-Driven Database through Platform-as-a-Service
- ▶ Host a Library Media Collection in the Cloud: From S3 to DuraCloud
- ▶ Use the Cloud for Library Instruction

In almost all aspects of the ways that libraries use technology, there are ways that it can make use of some flavor of cloud computing. While making the switch for major strategic systems requires careful consideration and broad-based institutional involvement, many opportunities remain where a library can try out and implement cloud computing on a smaller scale. In this chapter we will work through several practical projects that demonstrate the value of cloud computing, with some step-by-step guidance.

The services selected represent only a small sampling of the possibilities. In each category of service, there will be many other alternatives. No endorsement of the services is implied by citing them as examples. Services come and go on the market, and specific features and terms of service will likely change over time. Libraries will want to survey a wide range of available options as they consider implementation of cloud computing technologies.

▶LEVERAGE THE CLOUD FOR SUPPLEMENTAL STORAGE

Libraries can use cloud-based services for general-purpose file storage. Most libraries and similar organizations will have some type of systematic infrastructure for storing files, organized to provide shared folders for committees, teams, and work groups as well as for individual staff members. The data files created in the routine course of work at a library represent a valuable institutional asset. These files represent the accumulated work of the library's personnel, including such things as routine memos, budget and personnel administration, documentation of procedures, grant proposals and reports, committee minutes and documents, and all sorts of other activities. These collections of files and documents must be well organized, securely managed, and well protected from loss due to computer equipment failure or human error. For some libraries these documents may be considered public records and subject to inspection upon request. As a library considers whether to move its file storage to a cloud-based infrastructure, it will need to ensure that it maintains the proper levels of organization and control rather than slipping into more informal treatment. Replacing the systematic infrastructure for file management that might be in place on the library's local file server will take considerable planning and effort.

In addition to the formal institutional files and documents, libraries also deal with many computer files that can be treated more informally. At any given time, individual library staff members may need to have portable access to files related to current projects. Those that give presentations away from the library, that work on professional committees, or that collaborate in other ways with persons outside their organization need ways to exchange files outside the library's formal infrastructure.

This type of supplemental file access lends itself to cloud storage, with its inherent capabilities for portable and flexible access. Working copies of files can be deposited in a cloud storage service to provide convenient access that can be controlled as needed. This approach to cloud storage replaces practices such as sending files through e-mail attachments or carrying them on USB flash drives. Sharing files through e-mail attachments is a common practice but can run into difficulties with large files that may not be accepted by all mail systems. USB drives can be easily misplaced and offer very little security. Anyone finding a misplaced USB drive can gain access to its files, except in the rare instances where the owner takes the time to use some type of encryption.

Several cloud storage services are available that provide a convenient way for storing and sharing these types of supplemental files. One of the most popular services is Dropbox (https://www.dropbox.com/), which offers a modest amount of storage (2 GB as of June 2011) without cost, with paid subscriptions at levels of up to 100 GB. Dropbox offers a web interface to access and upload files as well as downloadable clients for Windows, Mac, and Linux that represents the user's cloud storage space as a folder on the computer. Any files copied into this folder automatically upload to Dropbox; files shared by others will appear. Dropbox allows files to be kept entirely private to the owner, shared with other individual users, or open to any user with an account.

When using cloud storage for supplemental files, it's important to be sure that the files are also deposited within the library's formal files systems when appropriate. While it may be convenient to use services such as Dropbox to share files, final copies should be stored in ways consistent with organizational policies. It's also prudent not to store the only copy of a file in a cloud storage service. While these services are generally reliable, they do not usually include backup and file restoration services.

Cloud storage services provide a flexible environment for sharing files with adequate security to ensure access only by intended recipients. Files can be shared among users of all types of computing environments, provided they have access to the Internet. Use of these services can be one of the easiest ways for a library to begin to investigate cloud computing.

Libraries can easily integrate cloud storage into their operations to facilitate the way they manage documents and files. Especially for library staff members who use different computers in the course of their work, Dropbox is a convenient service for convenient, centralized access.

The first step to set up Dropbox for file synchronization is to sign up for user accounts, which will be tied to each staff member's e-mail address. Keep in mind that only a limited amount of storage can be used under the free level of service, which should be sufficient for documents and spreadsheets but not necessarily for large numbers of images or video. After signing up, install the Dropbox client. It can be installed on both Windows and Macintosh computers and will create a folder that appears as any other on the local file system but that actually resides on the Dropbox servers.

Services like Dropbox support a variety of practical scenarios. A reference librarian, for example, can place active documents in Dropbox and also work on them during quiet periods when staffing the reference desk. Those who work from home or when traveling can likewise use Dropbox to keep all their work synchronized.

► USE GOOGLE APPS IN YOUR LIBRARY

Another way that a library can gain experience with cloud computing is to use web-based mail and document processing applications. The suite of applications from Google, for example, includes a variety of communications, collaboration, and office productivity tools that find wide use and increasingly displace desktop-oriented applications such as Microsoft Office.

Many organizations find it more efficient and cost-effective to take advantage of a web-based mail service provided by cloud services such as Google Apps than to operate their own mail servers, such as Microsoft Exchange or one of the many mail packages that run under Linux. Given the rampant volume of spam and malware, maintaining a mail service involves many layers of filtering and security in addition to the basic mail delivery features. Cloud-based mail services suit small organizations especially well, because they are unlikely to find it worthwhile to dedicate technology personnel and equipment to a routine service available at little or no cost from external providers.

To effectively use a suite of tools such as Google Apps in an organization such as a library, some considerations apply that would be different than for personal use. Many individuals maintain a personal mail account through Gmail or other providers in addition to their institutional account in order to separate personal correspondence from work matters. Gmail is a very popular option, although many other alternatives are available as well. After a simple, free registration process, you can begin sending and receiving e-mail and using Google's other services, such as Google Docs.

Organizational use of a web-based mail service takes a bit more effort than registering for a personal account. An e-mail carries an important element of identity for the organization, so it's helpful to have addresses that reflect the organization's domain instead of the generic "user@gmail.com." Some Google Apps are designed for various types of organizations, including commercial businesses, nonprofits, education, and government, that include the ability to use the organization's own domain name. A free version includes basic features for up to ten accounts. Those needing more accounts or wanting access to some of the advanced features will need to upgrade to the appropriate program, which may involve a monthly fee.

If your library is part of a larger organization, such as a corporation or university, your task may be more complicated, especially if you want to set up an organizational e-mail account just for the library and not on behalf of the broader entity. Libraries in this situation will need to carefully consider whether they want to establish their own separate organizational e-mail using something like Google Apps or if they want to participate in the enterprise system. As noted in Chapter 2, operating separately has some disadvantages relative to communicating with groups and users in the broader organization. Many large organizations have themselves shifted to web-based mail systems, mitigating the benefits that subordinate entities, such as libraries, might have in moving to their own separate cloud-based service.

To establish an organizational account, your library should have its own domain name. While it's possible to just use a set of individual accounts, bringing them together through a registered domain helps to organize the accounts and to facilitate easier communication and collaboration. Most libraries will already have a domain name, generally something like "my library.org." New domains can be purchased for a reasonable fee from one of the many registration sites (e.g., Register.com, GoDaddy.com, and Network Solutions.com). The most challenging problem with domain registration involves finding an available name that best describes your library. Domain names must be globally unique, and it's possible that another library with a similar name in another area already has the name you want or that the name has been snagged by someone hoping to make a profit.

Having a properly registered domain name will be necessary for other cloud-based services your library may want to use, such as a hosting service or a cloud storage provider. Although there may be a few technical details involved, it's worthwhile to understand how to register and configure a domain name for your organization. The domain naming system, or DNS, is one of the core principles underlying the Internet.

Once you have established your domain name, proceed through the following two steps to create your organizational Google Apps environment:

▶ **Step 1: Verify to Google that you own the domain name, and select a DNS service.** If you operate a web server with that domain name, you can choose the verification option that provides a file for you to deposit in its root directory. Once that file has been put in place, the second step of the process triggers Google to attempt to retrieve the file. If successful, Google has the evidence it needs that you actually own the domain and can use it as the basis for your organizational account. If you don't have a web server running at this domain, an alternative approach involves adding a TXT record to the DNS entry, which can be accomplished using the configuration tools of your domain registration provider. Figure 5.1 illustrates the domain verification feature of Google Apps.

To complete this step, you will select a DNS service, which will enable the Gmail servers to send and receive mail for your domain. As instructed by the Google Apps setup wizard, select the DNS service you want to use and then follow the instructions on updating the mail exchange (MX) records. These techniques may sound a bit complex but can usually be accomplished fairly easily, and Google provides clear instructions if you need help. After these technical tasks, all the remaining registration steps are done through simple menu options on the Google Apps account console. Figure 5.2 illustrates how the Google Apps configuration wizard presents the specific entries that you need to enter in your registration service; Figure 5.3 shows the page used by Register.com to enter this information.

► Figure 5.1: Verify Domain Ownership

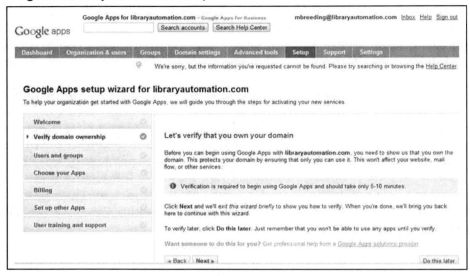

Although Google offers its web-based interface as the default way to read Gmail, it's possible to access mail in other ways. The library may want to enable those with smartphones to access their mail messages. Google's setup menus include an option to enable access to Gmail

► Figure 5.2: Setup Wizard

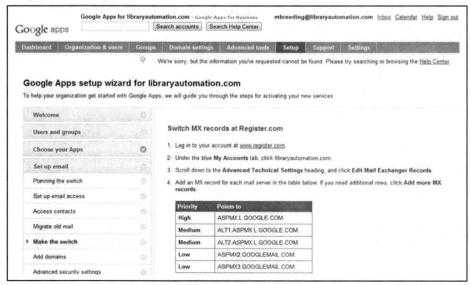

▶ Figure 5.3: Set MX Record in Register.com

using IMAP (Internet Message Access Protocol), which allows these devices to send and receive mail through their organizational accounts.

▶ Step 2: Set up groups and users. The free version of Google Apps allows up to ten user accounts. Creating groups will be helpful for sending messages to specific groups of users in the library. Groups can be set up for library administrators, standing committees, circulation staff, reference librarians, or any other set of personnel who regularly work together. These groupings can also be used for collaborative access to documents in Google Docs, which is automatically associated with your organizational account. Figures 5.4 and 5.5 illustrate the very simple processes for setting up users and groups in Google Apps.

▶ Figure 5.4: Create a New User

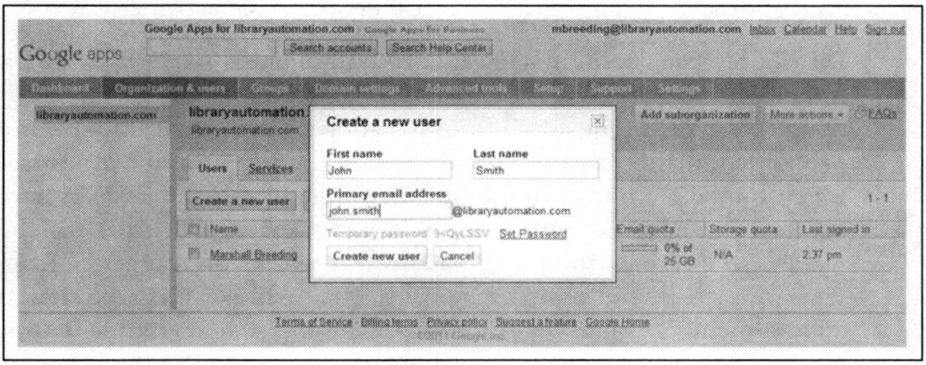

▶ **Figure 5.5: Create a New Group**

As you set up the accounts for the personnel in the library, you will want to follow a consistent pattern for the e-mail address and group names. Although you can change them later on, establishing some consistent conventions from the beginning will avoid confusion. It's quite common, for example, to create e-mail addresses in the form of firstname.lastname@mylibrary.org. This approach makes it easy for library personnel to remember each other's e-mail address, and it lends a more professional appearance than the use of nicknames that a given staff member might use in social networking or other informal settings.

Once you have established accounts for each library staff member, you can begin putting the service into use. Depending on the size of the library and staff's existing comfort level with services like Gmail, the implementation and training routine may be informal, or you may need to develop a more structured approach. In either case, cover these few basic activities:

▶ **Distribute e-mail account names.** Each staff member needs to know his or her e-mail address.

▶ **Assign passwords.** The administrator setting up the e-mail accounts will probably want to use the default preassigned temporary password, which can be given to each user for their initial log-in. Once users have successfully entered with their temporary password, they will be prompted to create their own password. It is accepted practice from security, privacy, and policy perspectives that passwords not be shared among members of an organization, including system administrators. System administrators have the ability to reset passwords should one be forgotten or if access is needed to the account in unusual circumstances, such as when a staff member leaves the organization.

▶ **Migrate e-mail from previous systems.** If your library has previously used a local mail server, such as exchange or the Unix mail utilities, you should migrate previous messages into your new service. Tools that allow an administrator to move all the mail accounts of an organization from an incumbent system to Gmail are available only to those subscribing to the paid educational or business accounts. The free version of Google Apps has the capability to move messages and folders from other systems one account at a time. To move mail from Microsoft Exchange, for example, a migration utility would need to be installed on the workstation of all staff members needing to move their account. Migrating messages from a previous mail environment increases the complexity of the implementation, but it can be accomplished if necessary.

▶ **Train users.** Library staff may need instructions on how to log in to their Google account and on how to make best use of its features. Some staff members may have personal accounts, for example, and will need to know how to log out of one account and into another. Those staff members who have used Gmail or other web-based mail systems may need very little training.

As the library implements Gmail, it will need to decide whether it wants to use the other components of Google Apps. As library personnel log in to their account, they will also be able to use Google Docs and the calendaring application. If your library already has a well-established environment for the way that it manages its documents, then it may not necessarily be advantageous to encourage personnel to use Google Docs, for example. Having some documents on the library's network file server and others in Google Docs can cause confusion. But if the library has not instituted a systematic environment for collaboration, then making use of this Google App may be advantageous. If, for example, most word processing files are simply stored on the local drives of individual staff workstations, where they may or may not be regularly backed up, shifting to Google Docs may be an easy path to a more systematic and secure business environment. Libraries ready to move most of their communications and productivity to the cloud will find that Google Apps provide a well-integrated environment.

Libraries that use Google Docs as their main word processing environment may want to institute some standard practices and conventions that will keep the organization's documents well organized. Documents by default are private so that only the owner can view or edit or even know that they exist. The real power of Google Docs comes from its ability to selectively share documents with other individuals or groups (see Figure 5.6).

▶ **Figure 5.6: Google Docs Collections and Sharing Features**

Google Docs allows documents to be organized into "collections." The administrator of the library's Google Apps account can create collections that correspond to departments, committees, or other work groups and establish sharing parameters according to the groups that were set up for Gmail, providing a convenient way for these groups to work together. Google Docs allows multiple individuals to edit a document at a time, so all team members can participate in the development of reports, documentation, and other group projects. Documents can also be shared with individuals outside the organization, a feature that can be helpful for working with professional colleagues on journal articles, ALA committees, or other collaborative projects.

▶ PROVIDE CLOUD-BASED E-MAIL ON A LARGE SCALE

Maintaining a mail service can require tremendous resources for a college or university with many thousands or tens of thousands of individuals in its community of students, staff, and faculty. An increasing number of colleges and universities find that operating a commodity service such as e-mail may not be a wise use of IT resources and the level of technical personnel required. Many universities have shifted these services from ones internally provided to outsourced arrangements. It's especially attractive to shift students to cloud-based e-mail services, because they represent a very large number of accounts that must be maintained, saving significant amounts of labor and technical infrastructure.

Large-scale implementation of mail, storage, documents, and other services through the cloud exceeds the levels of service that companies such as Google offer for free and move into programs such as Google Apps for Education or Google Apps for Business that involve costs on a per-user basis. The costs of these programs can represent significant savings on the expenses incurred, especially when taking into consideration the personnel and technical resources devoted to providing these commodity services locally.

Yale University, for example, announced in April 2011 that it would begin moving its mail and other services to the suite of Google Apps for Higher Education (see http://www.google.com/a/help/intl/en/edu/ index.html). Other major universities in the United States using Google Apps for Higher Education include Arizona State University, University of Notre Dame, and Northwestern University.

Microsoft also offers programs for education, including Office 365 Suite for Education, a new program replacing Live@edu, its previous offering for schools, colleges, and universities. This new program includes a basic set of free web-based services for students plus an advanced set of services for students, faculty, and staff at a low per-user cost.

Using a cloud service for e-mail and productivity involves placing the associated data outside the confines of the organization's local infrastructure, which in some cases may raise concerns of privacy and security. The data may include official institutional records and correspondence as well as the business and personal documents and correspondence of the individuals associated with the institution. The storage of such information in public cloud environments will require a high level of safeguards to ensure security, privacy, and integrity.

Institutions that take advantage of these outsourced, cloud-based services for their productivity applications need to ensure that their data receive equal or higher measures of security than they would provide in their local infrastructure. Security measures must be in place to ensure no unauthorized access. Multiple layers of data backup need to be implemented for disaster recovery of individual files damaged through human or technical error.

Use of outsourced services for e-mail and productivity comes with a variety of security and privacy concerns. In addition to general concerns for privacy regarding e-mail correspondence, documents, or data sets, there may be confidential, sensitive content and data subject to official regulation. The Health Insurance Portability and Accountability Act (HIPAA) of 1996, for example, specifies very stringent rules for access to patient data for organizations involved in health care (see http://www.hhs.gov/ocr/privacy/); The Family Educational Rights and Privacy Act (FERPA) establishes regulations regarding access to student records by educational institutions (see http://www2.ed .gov/policy/gen/guid/ fpco/ferpa/index.html).

The level of concern with these issues will depend on the size of the organization and the kinds of data involved. A small library moving to Google Apps, for example, will have far fewer concerns than would apply to a large university or corporation. Large or small, organizations considering shifting their business environment from local infrastructure to the cloud will need to carefully assess any applicable concerns with privacy, security, and policy.

▶ POWER A STATIC LIBRARY WEBSITE FROM THE CLOUD USING AMAZON S3

A library's website is one of the most visible and critical components of its technical infrastructure. It's essential for it to be fast, reliable, and flexible. Operating a website using cloud infrastructure can deliver these qualities without the overhead involved in maintaining a local server in the library.

There are many options available in the way that a library can operate its website. The possibilities are almost endless, but a few of the alternatives include the following:

- ▶ House a local server in the library. Common environments include Windows Server operating system using the built-in Internet Information Server, Linux, or Unix using the Apache web server.
- ▶ Use a colocated server. The library-owned server is housed in a data center of the higher-level organization.
- ▶ Use a fully outsourced hosting service; an external firm takes full responsibility for the hosting of the site. These arrangements may also include services related to the graphical design, layout, and navigation.
- ▶ Enter a specialized web-hosting arrangement based on a specific content management system such as Drupal. The hosting site maintains an instance of Drupal for the library along with the appropriate server infrastructure. The hosting arrangement may include services such as the initial Drupal layout, development of custom themes, and integration of any Drupal modules needed.
- ▶ Choose a cloud-based infrastructure in which the library manages the design and content of the site. In this arrangement, as we'll see in the following example, the library develops the content for the site and uses Amazon A3 to store and host the files that comprise the site.

Although we see that there are many different possibilities in how a library might support its website, an option that demonstrates the power and flexibility of cloud computing is to use Amazon's S3 service to host the files that comprise the site. In this example, we'll assume that the library has created the HTML files using a web-authoring product, such as Adobe Dreamweaver.

This approach works well for static websites. If your site relies on a content management system or is generated dynamically from database content using PHP or Perl scripts, other approaches will be better suited. The Amazon Simple Storage Services (S3) product provides a very high performance and reliable way to serve basic webpages. S3 can also be used to supplement dynamically generated websites, delivering images, style sheets, or any other static pages involved. If your site makes use of database and scripting environments, then you may need the full capabilities of a Linux or Windows server to host the site, which can be deployed through the Amazon EC2 service (discussed in the next section). Here, we'll assume a basic static website and proceed through the following seven steps to use Amazon S3:

▶ **Step 1: Create the website on a local workstation.** The workstation does not have to be configured to operate as a web server. You can use any web-authoring tools available that you are comfortable with. Make the site as simple or as complex as needed. As you create links to internal pages or images, be sure to use relative links that are not hard coded for a particular website URL. For example, use links such as:

```
<img src="/images/logo.jpg" />
```
   instead of:
```
<img src="http://www.mylibrary.org/images/logo.jpg" />
```
   [don't include a domain name]

By using relative links, pages created on your test or development environment will function properly once they are uploaded to your production Web server, such as the S3 service.

   You will also want to set up the same directory structure on your deployment server as your production environment, such as separate folders for images, style sheets, files, and the like.

   Test the site on the local workstation to ensure that it has the desired content and appearance and that the navigation works properly. In this scenario, the content will be developed on this deployment environment and transferred to the Amazon S3 service once ready.

▶ **Step 2: Sign up for an account on Amazon Web Services.** Amazon offers a variety of cloud-based services, including S3 for storing and providing access to files, EC2 for deploying servers in a public cloud, CloudFront for distribution of content stored in S3 in ways that meet the demands of very high-use web destinations, including the ability to deliver streaming video content, as well as many other more sophisticated services that come into play for organizations with very complex websites (see Figure 5.7). Our example makes use of S3, the most basic component of Amazon Web Services.

► **Figure 5.7: Amazon Web Services Main Page**

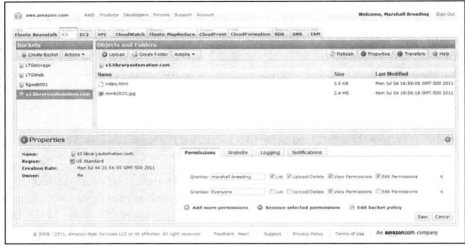

To sign up for an account, go to http://aws.amazon.com/. The sign-up process involves providing your e-mail address, contact information, and credit card number for any charges that apply. Even if you plan to stay within the free levels of service, you will need to supply payment information. A single registration process provides access to all of the components of Amazon Web Services. You will activate each product, such as S3 or EC2, individually as you need them.

To activate S3, you simply click on the "S3" tab after you log in to the Amazon Web Services management console, and then click on the "Websites" tab in the lower right pane (see Figure 5.8). You will be prompted for the e-mail address associated with your Amazon Web Services account. Next, you will be prompted for a phone number for the verification process. A four-digit pin number will display in the verification, which you will need to enter when you answer the telephone verification call, initiated immediately upon submission. If you successfully complete the verification process, the S3 service will be activated for your account and you can begin using it.

► **Step 3: Create a bucket to store the files that comprise the website.** The Amazon S3 service allows you to set up containers that it calls "buckets" to store files that you upload. In the right panel of the S3 management console, click the "Create Bucket" button. You will be asked to provide the name of the bucket and the region in which it should be created. The region represents the geographical area in which the bucket will be hosted, such as "US Standard." If your project

▶ Figure 5.8: Website Activation Section on the Amazon Web Services Main Page

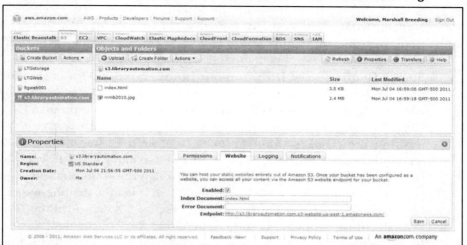

addresses users primarily in another continent or country, then you would select the appropriate region accordingly.

Pay careful attention to how you name the bucket that will be associated with your website. In most cases, the name should match the full domain name of your site, such as "www.mylibrary.org." Naming restrictions require that the name be unique within your region. Using your domain name should not be a problem, because it must be globally unique.

Once the bucket has been created you can create any folders needed to correspond to the structure of your website. In most cases you will want separate directories for images, style sheets, and other support files.

▶ **Step 4: Activate the bucket as a website.** To accomplish this task, select your bucket in the left panel, and, from the Actions dropdown menu, choose "Properties." The properties window that opens on the bottom right side of the page will include several tabs from which you select "Website." You simply check the "enabled" box and provide the name of the default document in the "Index Document" field, such as "index.html."

▶ **Step 5: Set the appropriate permissions and policies.** By default files are private to the owner. Under the "Properties" panel for your bucket, click the "Permissions" tab, add a new grantee with the name "Everyone," and check only the "View Permissions" box. Also on the Permissions panel, click on the "Add bucket policy" icon on the bottom right, which will open a box in which you will need to paste in the appropriate policy, which you can copy from the Amazon Web Services documentation, under the section "host your static websites," available from a link on the Website tab. The only change you will need to make from the sample policy will be to replace "example-bucket" with the name of your bucket that holds your website files.

► **Step 6: Configure the DNS.** You must configure the DNS so that the files are available through the library's domain name. Any bucket or file activated for web access through S3 will be available through a URL from Amazon's own domain, such as "https://s3.amazonaws.com/s3 .mylibrary.org/index.html." In order to make the files in the bucket served through your own URL, you will need to add a CNAME entry to your DNS configuration, implemented through the configuration page of your domain provider. For our example, we'll assume that the site will be accessed through "s2.mylibrary.org." Figure 5.9 demonstrates how to create the appropriate CNAME entry using the Register.com service. In the field preceding your domain name enter the subdomain that you will use, which in most cases will be "www." In the implementation phase you may want to use a CNAME such as "test" in order to work on the site unobtrusively. You will enter the Amazon domain appropriate for your bucket and region in the rightmost field, usually something like "s3.amazon.com."—including the period at the end of "com." Once you save entry on your domain service, it may take a few hours for it to take effect because it will need to propagate to other domain servers on the Internet.

► Figure 5.9: DNS CNAME Registration

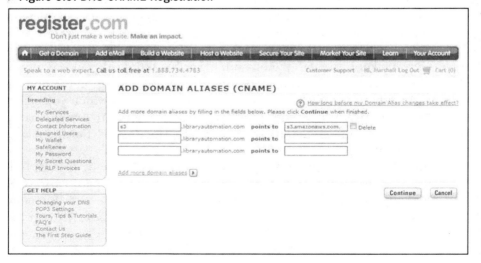

▶ **Step 7: Upload your files.** You are now ready to upload your files from your staging system to Amazon S3. The easiest way to accomplish this step is to use the built-in capability of the Amazon Web Services management console (see Figure 5.10). Third-party utilities, such as "Bucket Explorer," can be purchased that provide additional features for those who will make extensive use of S3. To upload the files using the console, simply click on your bucket's name on the leftmost panel, and choose the Upload function from the top middle panel. A window will appear that includes a button to "+ Add files," which when pressed allows you to navigate and select the files to be uploaded. Once selected, simply click on the "Start Upload" button on the lower right. You will need to upload all of the files in the root portion of your bucket and any subfolders according to the structure of your website.

You have completed the process of establishing service with Amazon S3. You are now ready to test and fine-tune your website. It should be available under both an Amazon.com URL and the one associated with your domain. Verify that all of your links work properly. If you find that the site works through the Amazon URL but not through your domain, you will need to verify the CNAME mapping configured through your registration service.

Once fully configured you will have a website hosted through a powerful and reliable platform. The cost for most library websites should be minimal and, unless your site has a very large number of files of substantial size or experiences extremely heavy use, may fall within the free levels of use.

▶ Figure 5.10: Upload Files

Hosting a static website provides a good introduction to infrastructure-as-a-service. Additional steps would include using Amazon's EC2 service to create a dynamic website or to support other components of the library's computing infrastructure that require the full capabilities of a Unix or Windows server.

Even if you cannot host your library's entire website through Amazon's S3 service, you may be able to use it for portions of its content, such as multimedia content that may be slow to load on a local server. If your library's connection to the Internet lacks sufficient bandwidth to deliver large image or video files with fast performance, shifting them to delivery through Amazon's S3 service can make a dramatic difference. To implement the delivery of selected content, you would follow the steps described earlier, creating a domain similar to "multimedia.mylibrary.org" that you would link from within your site's pages to the copies on S3 instead of your local server.

▶ POWER YOUR DYNAMIC LIBRARY WEBSITE FROM THE CLOUD USING AMAZON EC2

Many libraries have more complex websites that go beyond the use of only static pages. They use dynamic content generated through some type of internal database and scripting language, rely on a content management system, or have other components that require a full-fledged server.

Note that the EC2 service assumes a fairly high level of technical proficiency. It's not a turn-key web server but will require the same level of skill and effort as would working with a local server, less the parts of the process that involve hardware. The key advantage of using a service such as EC2 lies more in its higher performance, reliability, and potentially lower cost than operating a local server, not necessarily in reducing the technical expertise involved. Technology personnel used to working with operating systems such as Linux will find the operating environment familiar, although they will need to master some additional tasks specific to Amazon Web Services. An experienced systems administrator should be able to shift from working on local hardware to a cloud-based system such as Amazon's EC2 with a week or so of exploration, study, and practice.

As an example of using a virtual server provisioned through infrastructure-as-a-service, we'll step through the process of setting up such a server using the Amazon EC2 service. We will not describe all of the technical details involved at the level of the internal operating system but will work through the general concepts specific to this type of environment.

As for S3, to use EC2 you will need to create an Amazon Web Services account if you do not already have one. See the instructions earlier for the S3 service if needed. This account will be established with the contact information for the system administrator in your library, and you will need to provide payment information. Once your account is activated, work through the following steps:

▶ **Step 1: Activate the EC2 service.** Each of the products within Amazon Web Services needs to be activated separately. The first time you select the EC2 tab within the Amazon Web Services console, you will be prompted through its activation service. You will provide a telephone number, and the activation service will call and request the PIN code presented on the activation page. Once the EC2 service is activated on your account, you can begin to activate the server image that will support your web server.

▶ **Step 2: Activate a server instance.** The Amazon EC2 service essentially allows you to operate a server, using the operating system of your choice. Once you have activated your account for access to EC2, you can begin by launching what is called an Amazon Machine Instance (AMI), a virtualized server with complete computing and storage capabilities (see Figure 5.11). When launching the AMI, you will need to select the operating system and resources you need for your project. Amazon offers 750 hours of access to a Linux Micro Instance AMI within its free tier of service, which is adequate to operate a web server continuously all year. While the specific resources offered will change over time, the current Linux Micro Instance AMI includes 613 MB of system RAM on a 32- or 64-bit platform with 10 GB access to Elastic Block Storage. These resources should prove sufficient to power most library websites

▶ **Figure 5.11: Configure AMI**

with dynamic content applications. Amazon offers much more powerful server instances, which may be needed for some of the more complex applications that a library might run, but for the purpose of this example we'll work with the Linux Micro Instance.

We have selected the Micro Linux Instance for this example, because it is available within the free levels of service. Amazon offers many other instance types, including Red Hat Enterprise Linux, SUSE Linux, and different configurations of Microsoft Windows Server. The best one for your library will depend on the environment with which the technical personnel are familiar. Again, you will need personnel with the same degree of experience and expertise to manage these server instances in the Amazon cloud as would apply with managing these environments on local equipment.

Another part of activating an AMI involves establishing the key pairs that will be used for secure authentication. You create, save, and download a key pair file when you launch your AMI. This key will be needed to gain access to your AMI.

► **Step 3: Access your AMI.** You will access your AMI in the same way that you would access any other Linux system. One of the standard ways involves the use of a secure shell (ssh) utility such as PuTTY, which provides a command line connection into the server making use of encryption with strong keys to ensure that passwords or other sensitive information is not exposed. You will use the PuTTY Key Generator to import the key pair file that you created and saved associated with your AMI instance and then create and save a new a key pair file that will identify you; this will be created with a pass phrase that will be entered as you establish connections with the PuTTY client (see Figure 5.12).

► **Figure 5.12: Connect with PuTTY**

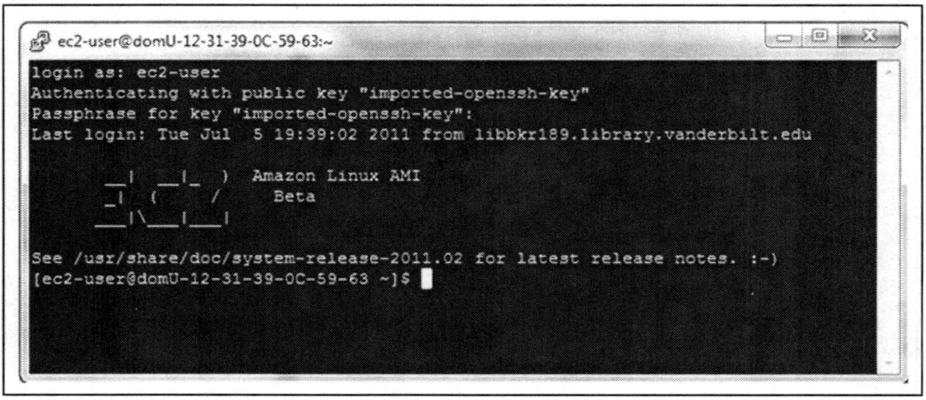

Once all these steps are complete, you should be able to connect to your new AMI as illustrated in Figure 5.13.

One of the key concepts to keep in mind with an AMI is its transient nature. By default no data or configuration information associated with the AMI persists when it is shut down or if something happens to crash the instance unexpectedly. Any permanent data needs to be housed through a volume in the Elastic Block Store or in an S3 bucket, which can be mounted to the file system in an AMI. It's essential that all data comprising the content of your website, configuration details, and especially dynamic database content be stored in some type of permanent storage within the Amazon Web Services environment and not in the transient file system of your EC2 instances.

Once you have your instance launched and have gained access to it through an ssh utility, you can begin building your website. The steps involved will depend on how your dynamic website has been designed and what components it requires. Some of the standard components that you will need to install and configure on your AMI include the Apache web server, a MySQL relational database, and the appropriate scripting languages, such as PHP or Perl. Depending on the type of instance from which you select when launching your AMI, the components of the stack you need for your server environment may or may not already be installed. If they are not present, you can use the standard procedures for installing and configuring them, which vary somewhat among the different Linux versions. We will not cover the details

▶ **Figure 5.13: View Instances**

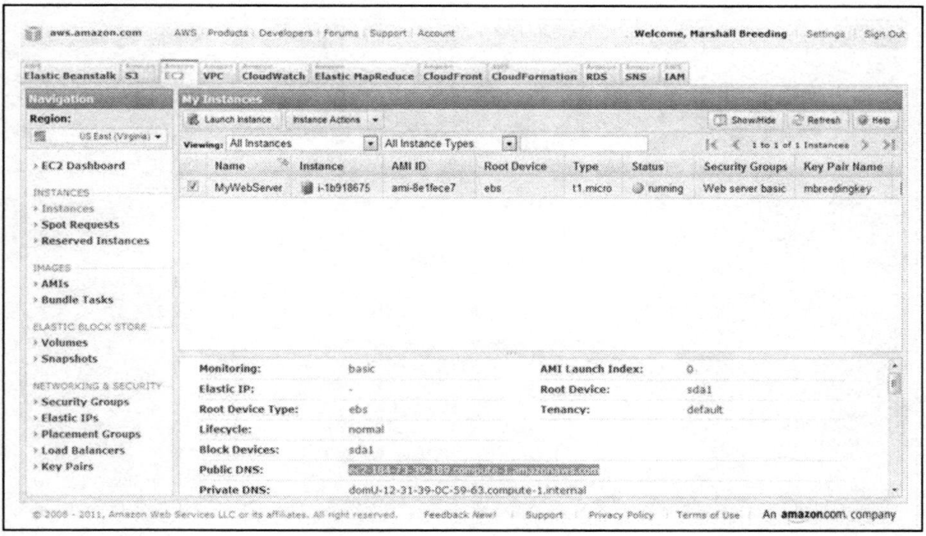

of these steps, which would be familiar to those familiar with Linux or Unix system administration and technically dense to others.

Once you have completed the installation of the components that you need to operate your server, you are ready to bring your data files into the environment. As noted earlier, it's important to store data files on permanent volumes from your Elastic Block Store. You will need to copy any HTML files and scripts into their respective directories and set permissions. If the site makes use of data stored in MySQL, you will need to install and configure MySQL and import the data.

Testing of the website can commence once the applications, modules, files, and databases are in place. This can be done by pointing a web browser to the Public DNS entry associated with your instance, specified in the description panel from the Amazon Web Services console. The security policies associated with your instance should be set to allow port 80 for your web server as well as any other TCP/IP ports that may be required for your content delivery environment.

Placing the server into production requires a few additional steps to make it available through your library's domain name. The Public DNS and associated IP address assigned to your AMI will change each time the instance reboots or is rebuilt, but you can request an Elastic IP address that is constant. The management console includes an entry under Networking and Security for "Elastic IPs," which launches a dialogue for Allocating an Address. Once allocated, it can be associated with your instance, as illustrated in Figure 5.14.

▶ Figure 5.14: Associate IP Address

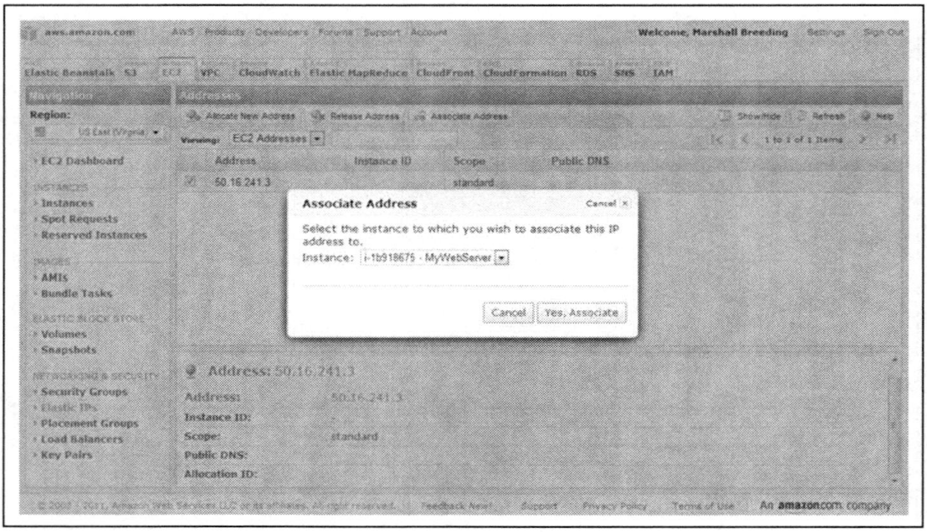

Once the Elastic IP has been associated with the instance, you can test access to your EC2-based website with this stable address.

The final step to creating your new cloud-based web server environment is to make the DNS change. Using the configuration console of your domain registration service, you will enter the address from the Amazon Web Service's Elastic IP associated with your instance to your library's domain name. This change will take as long as a few hours to propagate.

▶ POWER A WEB-DRIVEN DATABASE THROUGH PLATFORM-AS-A-SERVICE

We have seen how to implement a dynamic website based on the typical Linux, Apache, MySQL, PHP stack of components. This approach basically mimics the environment that would be installed on a local server but instead uses a virtual AMI. To achieve even more scalability and flexibility, or simply to experiment with other types of cloud technologies, a library could implement the database-driven website through platform-as-a-service (PaaS). Some of the popular services in this area include the Google App Engine and Amazon's Relational Database Service. PaaS services take the functionality of a database to a much more abstract level, separated from the constraints of being tied to specific machine instances. When running something like MySQL under an AMI in Amazon EC2, the developer or systems administrator must take care of many details in operating and optimizing the database environment. By using a database environment offered through PaaS, developers focus more on the data and building their application and less on lower-level tasks.

Library developers familiar with MySQL or Oracle will find themselves in somewhat familiar territory with Amazon's Relational Database Service (RDS). Database instances can be launched according to the requirements of the project. To launch an instance, the administrator would select the database engine, MySQL or the appropriate level of Oracle, the version and the class desired, and then enter some basic options such as the storage allocated to the database, and then assign names to the database and the username and password needed for access (see Figure 5.15). RDS automatically performs tasks such as backups, patch management, and database replication.

Once an RDS instance has been launched, it becomes available for use through any of the tools that programmers would use with MySQL in other environments. Using connectivity layers such as ODBC or DBI, applications and scripts can be written to create database tables, import data, and perform queries.

Amazon charges per hour for each RDS instance based on its class, data storage, and data transferred in and out. While access to MySQL installed

► **Figure 5.15: RDS Launch Instance**

under an EC2 instance can fall within the free levels of service offered, access to RDS will accumulate charges from its initial launch. RDS may be a good choice for high-use applications, providing a highly scalable database environment. Libraries interested in creating database-driven web applications based on MySQL might want to begin by developing the initial prototype using a machine-specific instance on an AMI and migrating to RDS as needed when the application is placed into production and experiences heavy use.

To take the construction of a database-driven application to an even more abstract level, a library could work with the Google App Engine, a true PaaS entirely abstract from any considerations of underlying hardware and operating systems. While RDS closely mimics the MySQL or Oracle relational database environments, Google Apps Engine takes a different approach. Its database component involves a structure oriented toward large comprehensive records instead of distributing data elements among multiple relational tables. Retrieving data is accomplished through the GQL query language, a variant of the SQL optimized for the data store of the Google App Engine.

Library developers will need to create their applications using one of the three supported programming languages: Python, Java, or Google's own Go. There are some tools to help transform existing applications into the Google Apps environment, but many of the basic assumptions of the Google Apps Engine differ significantly from the traditional server-oriented environment. Those wanting to try out the Google App Engine may want to work through some of the tutorials and code samples available and work up to building the specific applications that the library wants to create. The Google App Engine might be a good platform for basic tasks such as handling standard webforms on the library's website all the way up to sophisticated applications such as digital library management systems.

The basic approach to building applications with the Google App Engine involves installing the development tools on a local workstation and deploying the application in the Google cloud once completed. The development environment will vary according to the language used. To use Python, the programmer would first download and install the Python language on a local computer as well as an editor or integrated development environment (IDE). Next, download the Google App Engine SDK (software development kit) appropriate for your programming language and operating system, such as the Python SDK for Windows. You can also download an archived package of the documentation, or you can rely on the online documentation Google provides. To deploy your application you will need to create a Google account, if you don't have one, and register the application. The first time you register an account, you will need to perform a verification process that involves receiving a validation code through an SMS message to your phone number and creating a unique name for the application, which determines how it will be accessed in the Google cloud, such as "*libtechexample*.app spot.com." Once you have developed, tested, and deployed your application, you will be able to monitor how it is being used through the Google App Dashboard that was presented as an option in your Google account.

As with other cloud services, Google charges according to the resources consumed; a free tier of access is available within specified thresholds of use. Complete information on the Google App Engine is available from Google at http://code.google.com/intl/en/appengine/.

▶ HOST A LIBRARY MEDIA COLLECTION IN THE CLOUD: FROM S3 TO DURACLOUD

As libraries become increasingly involved in digital content, either through their own digitizing efforts or through licensed or purchased materials, the quantity of storage required may strain their local resources. These collections may include digitized images, often at very high resolution, digital photographs, streaming video, or digital audio files. Although disk drives of up to 3 TB are common and have become quite inexpensive, a more sophisticated infrastructure is needed for the storage, management, access, and preservation of these valuable digital assets.

Cloud-based infrastructure can provide additional alternatives in the way that a library hosts its rich media collections. Libraries manage their digital collections in many different ways. They may have a full-fledged digital asset management system such as DigiTool from Ex Libris or CONTENTdm from

OCLC, or they may have customized a multimedia repository using something like Fedora Commons.

Multimedia collections demand very special treatment in a library's technology environment, especially in cases where the objects may be unique. If a library has invested its resources into digitizing materials, extraordinary precautions must be taken to ensure their integrity and preservation. In dealing with these kinds of unique digital objects, a library needs to maintain several different copies, including the master file, contained in some type of trusted digital repository, as well as copies rendered in other formats for presentation or access. Image files are best preserved in loss-less formats such as high-resolution TIFF, but for viewing through the web surrogate copies in lower resolution JPEG or JPEG2000 can be rendered. In the absence of a full-fledged trusted digital repository that conforms to digital preservation standards and best practices, libraries will need to provide as much redundancy and security for the digital object files as possible.

In order to illustrate how to take advantage of cloud computing for support of a library's multimedia collection, we'll consider two examples. The first example will involve making use of Amazon's S3 and CloudFront services. Then we'll describe the DuraCloud service offered through DuraSpace, a relatively new organization created through the merger of the Fedora Commons and DSpace that provides a set of services related to the storage, preservation, and distribution of digital content based on distributed cloud storage.

An earlier example illustrated the power of the Amazon S3 service to provide a fast and reliable platform for storing files and delivering them through a web server. The same approach can also be used for multimedia content, although some important differences apply. The HTML pages that comprise a library's website tend to be tiny compared to the files that represent the digital objects of a multimedia collection. The total storage requirements for a basic website may be only a few megabytes and may even fall within the free levels of service offered by Amazon to be stored and delivered through S3. High-resolution images, digital videos, and audio files consume much more space, and therefore the cost considerations among storage options must be carefully evaluated.

One scenario that illustrates how cloud computing can support a library's multimedia collection would involve using the library's ILS to describe the materials and presenting links in the online catalog that connect library users to the content stored in Amazon S3. This approach may suit libraries that have a relatively small digital collection that do not yet have an extensive infrastructure such as a digital asset management system or digital preservation platform.

Three of the key activities that need to be addressed in putting together an environment for a multimedia collection include metadata management, storage and access of the digital objects, and attention to their security and long-term preservation. In each of these three areas the library has many options from which to choose. The approach that the library ultimately adopts will depend on the scale of the project, the level of funding available, and the time and skill sets that can be tapped among library personnel. Some may want to launch a prototype or proof-of-concept using existing resources or by taking advantage of free levels of service offered through cloud services providers. The following example may fit within this latter category.

To manage the metadata associated with the digital collection, a library could simply catalog the items in its ILS. While digital collections tend to be described using some profile of Dublin Core, some libraries use MARC records created in, or loaded into, their ILS. As long as the records are created consistently, they could be converted to Dublin Core should the library need them in this form for importing into a digital asset management system that it might acquire at a later time. But as a way to get started with systems that the library would already have in place, using the catalog module of the ILS to describe them is a reasonable way to get started.

In addition to the usual MARC tags that describe the item represented in the digital object, the linking field is the one most relevant to our example. Each record should contain an 856 field that contains the URL from which patrons can access the digital object. In this case, the URL will ultimately point to the object as it is served through Amazon S3. The library can either use the form of the link native to Amazon's servers, or it can be redirected through the library's own domain using the same CNAME technique described earlier.

The digital objects will be stored in an Amazon S3 bucket. The bucket will need to be created in the appropriate region relative to where the content will be accessed by your library's patrons. The buckets expand infinitely to hold the files represented by your library's digital collection. You can start with a few gigabytes worth of digital files to develop and test S3 as a component of the environment for your multimedia objects before ramping up to the complete collection.

The library will need to consider the cost factor of this approach. Given the larger size of multimedia digital files, the resources involved will quickly exceed the free levels of service. Amazon offers a web-based calculator to predict the costs of using its services (http://calculator.s3.amazonaws.com/calc5.html; see Figure 5.16). S3 cost components include the total storage as well as inbound and outbound data transfers. For pricing in effect in June 2011, the cost for storing 10 TB of data, with 200 GB estimated for moving files to the service and 100 GB for outbound traffic, totals $1,304.29 per month, or

► **Figure 5.16: Amazon S3 Cost Calculator**

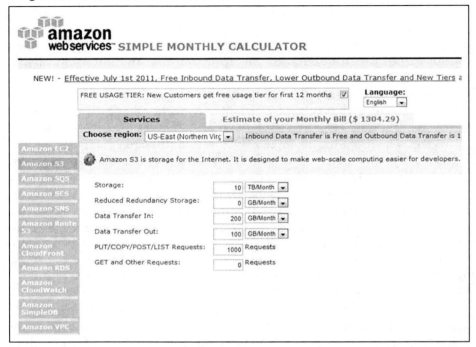

$15,651.48 annually, or $78,254.40 for a five-year project. As we noted in Chapter 3, the cost for cloud storage can be quite high for large collections. This cost cannot be compared against the price of basic disk drives but rather should be matched against all the components that comprise a complete storage environment, including the direct costs of either a Storage Area Network or Network Attached Storage, with at least Level 5 RAID (redundant array of independent disks), redundant RAID controllers and network cards, plus the indirect costs of the technical personnel to administer the systems, data center costs, and prorated costs of the network bandwidth consumed. While prices of raw disk drives continue to fall as their capacity increases, it's the surrounding infrastructure that accounts for much of the true cost of high-capacity storage.

As with any environment used to manage a digital collection, there will need to be a reliable link between the metadata records and the objects themselves. It will be necessary to copy the form of the link published through Amazon S3 into the subfield u of the 856 field in the MARC record. As the files are uploaded into S3, they will receive unique link addresses, which will serve as the connection between the metadata records and each digital file.

Another key issue involves how broadly you plan to provide access to the items in your collection. Will the items need to be restricted in some way, or is the library able to provide open access to everyone? Amazon S3 includes several options for controlling access. By default, objects stored in S3 remain private to their owner. For each bucket, its administrator can modify Permissions to allow others to access the files it holds. From the Amazon Web Services management console, select S3, choose a bucket, and then click on the Permissions tab. From here new levels of permissions can be added. Permissions can be granted other S3 users. For content that can be viewed openly, you would create a new permissions line granting View Permissions to the Grantee called "Everyone."

The library may need to restrict access to digital collections, such as allowing only on-campus viewing. S3 has the ability to limit access according to IP address through a bucket policy. You can limit access to the set of IP addresses associated with library or a college campus. To supplement IP access restrictions, you can also use its proxy server to provide off-campus access to its users through the username and password that they use for access to other restricted library resources.

Direct web access to files loaded on the Amazon S3 service usually provides an environment that's well beyond what libraries would be able to host locally in terms of performance and reliability. Amazon also offers a service called CloudFront, a content delivery network optimized for applications that distribute very large quantities of static and streaming content. CloudFront can take content stored in S3, or other origins, and deliver it from specific "edge locations" on the Internet able to deliver high volumes of content in a given geographic region. Few library-oriented applications would likely face the demands of very large numbers of users that services like CloudFront address.

Another layer that must be addressed in managing digital collections involves ensuring the security and preservation of the data files. All methods of storing computer files are vulnerable to failure. Local hardware or cloud-based storage services can experience problems that lead to data loss, including not only such events as hardware failures but also those caused by human error, software malfunctions, or malware attacks. It's essential to have multiple copies of all essential files and processes in place to ensure that backup files are up-to-date with the most current versions. Such backup practices are routine with an organization's business data. But very large digital collections that involve many terabytes of data require significant investments in redundant storage or tape media to accommodate multiple copies. We've noted the high cost of storing 10 TB of files on a service such as Amazon S3. Storing duplicate copies in multiple S3 buckets provisioned in different regions would be a convenient backup strategy but an expensive one. Other alternatives might entail keeping multiple copies on inexpensive USB drives housed locally.

A new service called DuraCloud (http://duracloud.org/) offers a more sophisticated approach to using cloud technologies for projects such as hosting a library's digital collections. DuraCloud was developed and is operated by DuraSpace, an organization that grew out of the merger of DSpace and Fedora Commons. Based on open source software, DuraCloud provides an interface that allows an organization to easily upload its content, which is then distributed to one or more cloud-based storage services, including Amazon S3, Rackspace, and Windows Azure. It also includes services related to validating the integrity of each file, synchronizing versions as needed, and creating any derivative transformations needed, such as converting TIFF master copies to JPEG. DuraSpace also offers a package of services related to public or controlled access to the items in the collection such as serving still images or streaming video. DuraSpace launched DuraCloud as a production service on November 1, 2011.

► USE THE CLOUD FOR LIBRARY INSTRUCTION

In addition to the types of resources that can be implemented using cloud technologies, libraries can also consider how some of their broad programs can make use of these services to facilitate their work.

Library instruction especially lends itself to the use of cloud technologies. Instruction sessions can be given in venues outside the library where resources that depend on its internal network are not conveniently accessible. Focusing on cloud-based applications will result in a repertoire of resources that attendees can conveniently access as they perform their subsequent research projects. By using an assortment of these web-based services, your library's instruction program can become more engaging and interactive. Some of the specific resources that can be employed to support library instruction programs are mentioned here.

Google Docs can be used collaboratively for tasks such as developing the content to be covered in each instruction session or organizing the roster of the courses and sessions that will be offered. Schedules for instruction sessions and related activities can be coordinated using the Google Calendar. If your library prefers attendees to register for instruction sessions, Google Forms provides a convenient way to set up a form that can collect this information.

Many instruction sessions begin with some type of survey that serves as a pretest or as a tool to gather information about topics that need to be covered. Services that could be used for this activity include SurveyMonkey (http://www.surveymonkey.com/), a full-featured survey instrument. Poll

Everywhere (http://www.polleverywhere.com/) provides a less complex service more appropriate for a quick preliminary poll more than a more complete pretest. With Poll Everywhere, the instructor creates the poll through a web interface and the attendees respond on their mobile phones, through Twitter, or on a computer through a web browser. Poll Everywhere offers a free level of service for less than 30 responses, with paid subscriptions at different levels based on increased numbers of responses per poll and additional features. Figure 5.17 shows a sample poll created using this web-based service.

Instruction sessions might need to demonstrate one or more of the content services or databases that the library offers. Librarians conducting the session might do a live demonstration, or they may prefer to use a video produced by capturing the use of the service through a screencasting service. Camtasia Studio from TechSmith is a commercial full-featured package with recording and editing tools. TechSmith offers educational discounts and a free trial period but no free levels of service after the trial period. Some free tools are available with a simplified set of features, such as the open source CamStudio (http://camstudio.org/). Links to screencasts of popular resources can be provided in subject resource pages to supplement other help or documentation for the resources.

Wikis have become a well-established media in which to develop content resources through informal collaboration. In contrast to many intranet platforms such as Microsoft SharePoint, a wiki can be set up with minimal effort, with as many or as few restrictions on contributing content as desired. In support of a library instruction program, a wiki could be established that offers a page or section on each of the sessions offered or disciplines covered. Although specialized commercial tools provide similar functionality in a

▶ Figure 5.17: Poll Everywhere

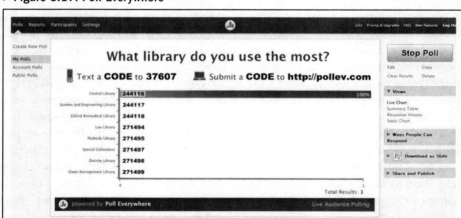

more prepackaged form, libraries not able to purchase these products can use a wiki to gain much of the same capacity.

Commercial subscription services such as Springshare's LibGuides fall well within the genre of cloud technologies, providing a platform that libraries can use to develop subject guides and other types of resources to benefit patron research (see http://www.springshare.com/libguides/index.html). Springshare offers a variety of subscription-based products designed to provide specialized support for library activities. LibGuides is a content management environment designed to help librarians create subject guides for each specialized discipline. It is delivered through SaaS, with all data stored on Springshare's servers. Libraries that subscribe to LibGuides are able to set up templates to give each guide a consistent layout and organization and to customize it to be consistent with the color scheme, branding, and navigational headers of its broader environment.

We've noted that many products with only marginal technical credentials promote themselves as cloud-based technologies. Springshare's products clearly embody all the characteristics of multitenant SaaS, yet its website and other marketing materials do not emphasize their technology foundation but rather their features and functionality. Springshare's matter-of-fact approach to delivering its products through web-based SaaS further illustrates how this approach to cloud technology has become a well-accepted mainstream technology. Springshare also offers LibAnswers, a platform for providing reference services via the web and SMS, with a knowledge base of answered questions.

Many other cloud-based services can also be incorporated into instruction sessions. Presentations can be enriched with images from photo-sharing sites such as Flickr, taking advantage of appropriate Creative Commons licenses; communications channels can be established through Facebook, Twitter, or Skype; and video library tours can be produced in advance and shared through YouTube. An appropriate sprinkling of these web-based services can result in a more engaging instruction session, as well as help cast the library and its librarians as savvy with current tools and technologies. Overuse of these services or bringing in sites that might have fallen out of the mainstream can have the opposite effect, so it's important to continually review and renew the tools selected for these sessions and to make sure that they are used strategically to enhance the presentation and not to dominate the session.

This chapter has described just a few of the ways that a library can put cloud computing to practical use. The examples cover a range of library scenarios and make use of different cloud technologies, including SaaS, IaaS, and PaaS as well as some general web-based services. We aim to give a taste of some of the possibilities and convey the general level of expertise and effort required to implement real projects based on these technologies.

►6

MARKETING

- ► **Market to Library Patrons**
- ► **Market to Library Personnel**
- ► **Market through Usability and Findability**
- ► **Use Search Engine Optimization**

As libraries develop their strategy to implement a new service or product, they should include a marketing component to ensure it gains the desired levels of use and attention. Any of the affected stakeholders should be well informed of changes underway. Entirely new services deserve special marketing efforts to be sure that its potential users become aware of what's now available to them and understand its advantages and benefits. An effective marketing plan will help ensure that the services of the library find their intended audience and hopefully gain the levels of use anticipated.

In the case of cloud technologies, marketing can take a number of forms. Some projects involving cloud-based technologies target the library's end users while others involve only library personnel. In this chapter we will consider active marketing efforts that heighten awareness of the service by library patrons as well as indirect marketing through improved usability and findability. We'll also discuss the different points of emphasis that apply to promoting the services to library staff versus library patrons.

►MARKET TO LIBRARY PATRONS

At the most basic level, the library should not have to market to patrons whether or not it uses cloud technologies. The technology choices that a library makes as it deploys its services should be completely transparent to library users. Few patrons will take an interest in what behind-the-scenes technologies support the services they experience on the library's website or within its physical premises. Given the ubiquity of these kinds of services that pervade other aspects of their experience, promoting something new in the library as based on cloud technologies may not necessarily come off as impressive.

As the library deploys new services based on cloud technologies, it's the services themselves that should be the focus of marketing to patrons and not their technical foundation. Libraries should avoid the temptation to characterize new services as being cloud based, because that term does not necessarily help spark their interest or help them understand its benefits. Details regarding the technologies or architectures, and even the product names that underlie a new service, tend to obscure the marketing effort.

New projects based on cloud technologies would therefore make use of the same marketing techniques as would any other new endeavor. Some of the basic components of a patron-oriented marketing plan might include the following phases.

First is to perform market research to validate the need for the service and to help shape how it will best be deployed. Activities in this phase might include an environmental scan of the options and opportunities in this area and how other libraries have addressed the issue; surveys to gauge demand for the service within the library's clientele; and focus groups that can exploit more sophisticated interactions to document the specific needs and requirements.

As the project nears completion, the library may want to engage interested patrons as early adopters of the service. These early reactions can provide important clues as to whether the product or service fulfills the anticipated needs as documented in the market research phase. These early adopters can help fine-tune the functionality, uncover errors or bugs in the technology, and provide other helpful feedback at a point in time when issues can be resolved with minimal disruption compared to after the service has been placed into production.

Once the timetable has been established of when the finished product will be placed into service, the library can begin a more active publicity campaign to promote awareness and to boost interest and use. Some components of this publicity plan might include the following:

▶ Incorporate the service in library instruction sessions. These sessions provide an important point of contact between librarians and patrons. While not all library services can be covered in an instruction, special attention might be given to new services that the library wants to promote.

▶ Train library personnel to direct users to the new service as needed as part of other service activities, such as in service desk interactions. Library personnel must be supportive of the new service and be willing to encourage its use by patrons when it suits their research tasks.

▶ Distribute promotional literature that provides details of the service. Depending on the type of service, printed brochures may be helpful for publicity. Brochures can be distributed at student centers or other popular venues or mailed to targeted recipients. Other collateral materials include pens, bookmarks, or business cards imprinted with the bare essential information, such as its name and URL.

▶ Devise an advertising campaign to heighten awareness in appropriate media relative to your clientele: student newspapers, ads on campus websites, links from the library section of courseware pages. A blitz of web-based ads, especially on sites frequented by library patrons, will help build awareness of the new services.

▶ Social media provide one of the best opportunities for publicity of library services. You can feature new library services on a Facebook page. Twitter can direct users to the service through inward links. To use social media effectively for a given purpose such as promoting a new service, the library must already have in place a strong social media strategy. It takes time to build Twitter followers or to gain engagement on Facebook, and these media can be effective marketing tools for a given project only if they have already been established as strong points of engagement for the library.

▶MARKET TO LIBRARY PERSONNEL

In addition to the publicity a library might direct to the end users of its services, it also needs to promote new services and technologies to the personnel who work in the library. It's unrealistic to expect library personnel to enthusiastically promote a new service or technology to patrons unless a process has been followed to earn their buy-in. Project planning needs to engage library personnel at the earliest phases of the project not only to elicit their support but also to tap the expertise and experience of the broadest range of perspectives represented in the library.

Library personnel need to be well informed regarding any new applications or services that they use directly in the course of their own work, but they also need to be familiar with the services available to patrons so that they can provide assistance. It's also important to ensure library personnel have a positive outlook regarding new services; early involvement should help promote the buy-in necessary to ensure the success of a project.

One aspect of marketing new applications based on cloud computing to personnel will involve education and awareness of this approach to technology relative to other models with which they may be more familiar. Those not familiar with the concepts that we have covered in this book initially may not be comfortable with the data related to their work being stored in some distant cloud-based service rather than on more tangible local devices.

One thread of marketing cloud computing to library personnel may revolve around the idea that it opens up to them a much wider range of tools to support their work than the library could ever provide on its own. Instead of having to wait for the library's IT department to implement a new piece of software that they may be interested in for their work, there may be a free cloud-based service available instantly. Cloud computing can also be empowering to those who don't consider themselves adept with technology. Many of the web-based services assume no particular technical skills and are designed to be set up and operated by individuals with the proficiency levels typical of most library personnel outside of the systems or IT department. Cloud computing lowers the thresholds of difficulty that accompany powerful applications so that library personnel can do their work with fewer obstacles. Emphasizing points such as these can be part of a program to educate and promote the use of cloud computing for library workers.

► MARKET THROUGH USABILITY AND FINDABILITY

Traditional marketing involves proactive activities to help library users become aware of a service that they might not have otherwise known about. These tactics help generate interest in the short term, but new services must also become part of the environment that library users come across in the course of their ordinary activities and simply use as one of the obvious choices presented to them. Building natural pathways that lead users to the service in the course of using the resources to which they are acclimated may bring many more users to the service than would a marketing campaign. As the library launches key new services, whether based on cloud computing or any other technology, they should be presented in such ways that they will be easily used regardless of special external promotion.

The library might conduct usability testing on two fronts. One set of studies might be designed to measure whether patrons will easily discover the service within the library's web presence. Are there obvious natural pathways that lead users into the service in the relevant scenarios? Or do they have a hard time finding the service or recognizing that it's the tool that will help them with the task at hand? Other usability studies would focus on the design of the service itself. Once users enter the service, can they use it effectively without advice and instruction? Usability studies can be conducted during an early adoption or preview stage so that adjustments can be made in response to any problems revealed.

▶ USE SEARCH ENGINE OPTIMIZATION

Another powerful way to market a new service lies in increasing its visibility through search engines. A strategy of search engine optimization attempts to lead users to the website or service through the major search engines, especially Google because it currently dominates in this arena. Because so many individuals rely heavily on search engines, it's vital for a library's resources to be well represented in their indexes and to be designed in such a way that they will be positioned favorably in search result lists.

Designing a web-based resource to be well placed in search results is part of a strategy of search engine optimization, or SEO. The key goal involves designing and implementing a site in ways that increase user interest through improved performance in the major search services. Two of the components of search engine optimization involve ensuring that the content from the site or service finds its way into the indexes of the search engines and that the content is presented in such a way that the relevancy algorithms of the search service will rank it highly relative to the appropriate end-user search queries. Search engines regularly scour the web to find all the sites to include in its index. Without any specific intervention, most of the search engine harvesting bots eventually will find new sites so that they are eligible to be included in search results. Search engine optimization aims to decrease the time it takes for the site to be indexed and to do as much as possible to make the site appear at the beginning of the search results. Some of the general techniques include the following:

- ▶ Provide clear, interesting, and authoritative content. Libraries have an abundance of information and should be able to position it in such a way that draws the attention of search engines. The content should be written and presented to best serve its human users. Any manipulation of content to manipulate search engines will likely hamper positive placements of results.
- ▶ Keep the HTML coding as simple and clean as possible. Search engines may have a hard time finding the key text of a page if it's buried within a complex morass of JavaScript and formatting directives. Handling formatting through separate style sheets can both simplify the coding of a page and foster a consistent presentation across all the pages in a site.
- ▶ Supplement clearly written, clean pages with metadata to help search engines understand the content of your site and present it better in search results. The two most important tags include the <title>, which should be short and unique for each page within your application, and <description>, a short summary of the content on the page, peppered

with strong keywords that highlight key content, concepts, or ideas represented on the page. Any attempt to manipulate the metadata tags in ways inconsistent with the text presented to human users can result in your application being removed from the search engine's indexes entirely.

▶ Give each page within the application a simple, clear, and persistent URL. To the extent possible, avoid cluttering the URL with session tokens and other parameters that may confuse search engine bots attempting to harvest your site.

▶ Create a sitemap, according to the specification of Sitemaps.org (http://www.sitemaps.org/), to provide search engine harvesters with a definitive list of the unique pages within your site or application.

Other factors that impact how well your site will perform in search engines include longevity, the number of other sites linking to your pages, and how often users actually select your pages in search results.

The basic strategies for search engine optimization apply whether your site or application relies on local infrastructure or is deployed through a cloud service. One consideration with cloud-based applications involves ensuring that the content becomes closely associated with your library and not the service through which it is deployed. The techniques that we noted in Chapter 5 for operating a service based on Amazon Web Services that redirect cloud-hosted applications through the institution's own domain name would be important to implement for search engine optimization as well as for the clarity they give to users regarding the source of the content.

All of these techniques contribute just as much to the health of your site or application for its intended audience as they do to improving search results. By following these practices, you can draw just as much use into your application organically as you might accomplish through other types of marketing efforts.

►7

BEST PRACTICES

- ► **Be Adventurous**
- ► **Try Before You Buy**
- ► **Proceed with Caution**
- ► **Guard Your Data**
- ► **Consider Long-Term Total Cost of Ownership**
- ► **Play by the Rules**
- ► **Jump into Trendy Technology Only as It Meets Strategic Objectives**

Other chapters have worked through some of the technical and practical definitions of cloud computing and have given many examples of how this approach to technology can be implemented to help support library activities. In this chapter we will highlight a few additional ideas and present some practical tips regarding some ways to get the most out of the technology and to warn about some of the pitfalls to avoid.

►BE ADVENTUROUS

Cloud computing lends itself to experimentation. With the conventional local computing model, there's an incredible amount of work involved with trying out new software. You have to gain access to a server, download and install the software, and go through a complicated configuration process before you can use it. Some of the perquisites may involve direct costs, which may hinder or delay the process. This model of computing discourages experimentation. You have to be quite sure that the software meets your needs before you invest the time, money, and infrastructure.

Cloud computing, on the other hand, makes very few demands up front. You need not worry about any of the behind-the-scenes infrastructure and can almost always get started with no financial investment. Almost all the cloud-based services offer a free tier of service, an introductory trial period, or other opportunities to try the service without risk or cost.

This low threshold of entry opens the possibility of trying out lots of different competing alternatives within a product category before making a final decision regarding which one to place into regular use. Traditional applications requiring thicker implementation processes demand significant advance research based on product brochures, documentation, and specifications and rarely does a library have an opportunity to install and use multiple alternatives before choosing one. Cloud computing turns this process upside down, allowing the library hands-on experience with several competing services before it makes a final selection.

Cloud computing also facilitates a more experimental approach in the way that a library gets involved in its own development projects. We've seen that through IaaS offerings like Amazon's EC2, a library can quickly launch virtual server images, storage, and other tools necessary to set up a development environment, usually at free levels of service. This instant access to free computing resources makes it much easier to quickly ramp up an environment to create, test, and prototype an application in response to a new idea or to solve a problem. By lowering the threshold of effort and investment, library development can be much more experimental. This kind of environment makes it feasible to quickly create a service or utility just to see if it might be useful and not have so much invested in it that it has to be placed into production. Lower thresholds of entry should translate into more ideas seeing the light of day, some of which don't work out and others that might prove to be valuable innovations.

▶ TRY BEFORE YOU BUY

Along the same lines, cloud computing allows a library to be more confident about the products it chooses to purchase, because it can use them for free before making a commitment to purchase. Once a smaller group has identified a general need and made an initial selection regarding the best service to address the problem, it's often possible to set up a free trial that can be fully configured with the library's own data. During this trial period, a wider set of stakeholders, including both library personnel and patrons, can put the service through its paces before a final purchase decision.

This more experimental and casual approach to many cloud-based services does not necessarily apply as much to large-scale business applications, such as ILSs, enterprise planning systems, or learning management systems. Even those offered through SaaS generally do not offer the free levels of service or trial periods seen in more lightweight applications. These types of applications tend to be quite sophisticated and involve complicated installation procedures, and even though cloud computing may be able to moderate the complexity, few vendors of these library-specific high-end products offer the same levels of free access as seen in other areas.

▶ PROCEED WITH CAUTION

Cloud computing necessarily brings a higher level of dependence on the company or organization providing the service. With locally installed hardware and software, a system continues to operate even if its developer experiences difficulties or even goes out of business. Such is not the case with cloud computing. Services can suffer an immediate impact due to technical problems or business issues. As libraries engage with cloud-based services they need to do so based on strong evidence that the services will be available at required levels for as long as needed. The terms of service within a license agreement or contract address these concerns but may not necessarily fully guarantee against disruptions or unplanned terminations. While the terms of service may offer some amount of financial compensation if the service does not perform to expected levels, it may not adequately represent the cost of disruptions to the library's core services and internal operations. Arrangements such as SaaS for strategic library infrastructure demand a higher degree of confidence in a vendor than applies to locally installed software.

It's ironic that in many ways cloud computing reduces risk and costs but once implemented for major applications results in a higher level of dependency on the provider. Overall this approach offers lower thresholds of entry but with higher stakes at risk on the performance of external organizations.

▶ GUARD YOUR DATA

Regardless of the technical deployment model, libraries have enormous investments in their data and should take all reasonable precautions to ensure its integrity, security, and preservation. Almost all forms of cloud computing result in your library's data being hosted externally. The library must take responsibility for its data, implementing all necessary procedures to meet or exceed the layers of precaution that would be in place if it were housed within its own infrastructure. Sufficient copies should be maintained to ensure recovery in the event of any type of failure. In some cases supplemental backup and recovery services may be part of the business terms specified in a subscription license or contract; it's also possible that the library will need to set up its own processes and procedures, such as the replication of data to alternate storage providers or by implementing automated scripts that copy data to local storage media. All contracts with service providers should clearly stipulate that the library maintains ownership of its data and can gain access to that data when use of the service is discontinued regardless of circumstance.

▶ CONSIDER LONG-TERM TOTAL COST OF OWNERSHIP

Libraries almost always deal with constrained budgets and must carefully choose how they invest their resources. It's therefore important to consider all angles of cost, including not only savings in the short term but especially the total cost of ownership throughout the expected life of the service. Earlier chapters have noted the budget implications of cloud computing, generally involving an all-inclusive higher monthly or annual subscription fee that offsets a variety of expenses that would apply with local implementations: capital costs and service plans for hardware; licensing fees for operating systems and applications software; fees for maintenance and support for the application; technical personnel for the administration of the server, operating system, database engine, and application; and facilities costs associated with a data center. As a library evaluates large-scale projects, especially large-scale business applications, it should develop budget models that project costs for each conceptual model and for each specific product under consideration for at least a five- to seven-year term. Although costs will not be the only prevailing concern, one component of the decision-making process should include a realistic view of the budget impact of competing scenarios.

▶ PLAY BY THE RULES

Cloud computing presents the opportunity for the library to bring in external services that can become part of its operational infrastructure. Many libraries also exist within larger entities and participate in systems and services provided for use throughout the organization. Components of such enterprise infrastructure span functions including e-mail and other communications media, network file storage, centrally managed websites, authentication and authorization services, and business and financial systems.

There exists a natural tension between individual units, such as a library, and the IT services provided at the broad organizational level. In a large organization, services tend to be delivered in standard ways that can't always be adjusted to the preferences of each part of the organization. Support for centralized services may seem weaker than individual departments would be able to provide for themselves. Yet, this enterprise approach to technology allows large organizations to operate more efficiently as a whole, taking advantage of economies of scale and reducing the equipment, environmental, and personnel costs compared with the redundancy involved in each department operating its own independent infrastructure services.

As a library begins to experiment and implement various cloud computing services, it's tempting to pull away from some of these centrally provided services. Implementation of new cloud technologies should not be done at the expense of disrupting the library's place within its larger enterprise. Moving library personnel from an institutionally provided mail system to a separate Gmail environment, for example, might be counterproductive relative to communications with the broader organization.

This principle of cooperating with centrally provided computing infrastructure does not necessarily result in constraint on the use of cloud-based applications. Libraries are involved with many varied activities not covered by centralized systems. Library-specific business applications such as ILSs, electronic resource management systems, OpenURL link resolvers, discovery interfaces, and the like would remain within the library's discretion even when supported by the central IT department. These library-specific systems interact with enterprise systems in ways that may require specific integration layers with close cooperation among library personnel, systems providers, and central IT staff. Any of the many smaller-scale services available through cloud computing providers can be implemented with no friction with central IT departments.

Libraries that operate independently of larger organizations enjoy much more freedom in the way that they assemble their infrastructure and will likely find that cloud-based services provide a much easier technology strategy than maintaining their own local infrastructure components. But even within these more independent libraries, it's important to abide by organizational concerns. Individual departments may find similar temptations to branch out on their own, taking up cloud-based services instead of using the infrastructure in place for the broader library organization. The same caveats apply. A fragmented approach where some individuals or departments use external services instead of that provided for the organization can be problematic.

The ease and flexibility inherent in cloud computing can evoke a tension between the urge toward innovation and responding quickly to demonstrated service needs and the need to operate within the bounds of organizational concerns. Cloud computing can spark some grassroots innovation in response to organizational sluggishness. By attending to the broader organizational issues and working within established channels, those interested in innovative use of cloud computing technologies can move forward without causing friction or running into barriers.

▶ JUMP INTO TRENDY TECHNOLOGY ONLY AS IT MEETS STRATEGIC OBJECTIVES

When shaping the technology strategy of a library, it's important to select products and services based on how they support its specific objectives and broad strategies. While it's important to gravitate toward computing platforms consistent with broad trends, a library shouldn't necessarily opt for a technology just because it's trendy. While cloud computing clearly stands as a mainstream approach, the hype of any given product may be difficult to distill from the practical advantages and disadvantages.

One of the chief reasons why cloud-based products or services might appeal to libraries would be their alignment with the realities libraries face in terms of personnel and financial resources. The broad character of cloud computing involves buying into infrastructure provided externally rather than relying on computing resources owned and supported directly. It's essentially outsourced information technology services. Libraries that lack their own in-house technical personnel may find SaaS and other cloud-based products well suited to their needs. Those that have more abundant resources, including staff members with technology skills and budgets that support the up-front costs of computing hardware, may gain advantages through working with locally installed systems. Of course, it's possible to mix and match, outsourcing some aspects of the library's environment to the cloud to free up time and talent to focus on specific projects that might benefit from local expertise.

Within this context the balance of pros and cons centers on basic issues of allocation of resources. Chapter 3 took a closer look at the budget planning issues. A cost versus benefit analysis should be an important driver in whether or not a library moves all or part of its technology support to the cloud.

These are just a few of the tips and observations that might lead to more successful use of cloud computing in a library. In general, libraries should apply the same kinds of decision making, change management, and strategic planning to cloud computing as they would with any other technology issue. While cloud computing brings in its own set of characteristics, it's also just the latest round of a constantly evolving technology scene.

▶8

METRICS

- ▶ Measure Use with Multiple Services
- ▶ Assess Strategic Impact

Libraries generally embrace a culture of assessment in which each of the services they offer is subject to objective measurement that must provide data that demonstrates its positive contributions to the libraries' strategic activities. Cloud-based applications fortunately are subject to a number of complementary approaches to gathering data regarding their use that can be analyzed in ways that help the library understand their effectiveness and impact. In this chapter we will take a brief look at some of the ways that libraries can collect usage data related to the cloud-based services they implement.

▶MEASURE USE WITH MULTIPLE SERVICES

Given that one of the fundamental characteristics of cloud computing involves allocating costs based on resources consumed, these products generally have extensive capabilities for recording many different usage metrics. Most cloud services include a management console that includes tools that monitor real-time use and cumulative statistics.

Amazon Web Services, for example, offers detailed reports on the resources used by all of the services activated under each user account. Aggregated numbers are provided as part of the monthly billing statement. Much more detailed data are available for download, offered in both CSV (comma separated values) files, suitable for importing into spreadsheet applications such as Microsoft Excel, and XML files, which can be parsed and imported into any statistical application.

A number of third-party tools are available for analyzing usage statistics from Amazon Web Services. CSS Corp., for example, has developed an open source application called CloudBuddy Analytics that presents detailed reports on the use of S3 buckets (see http://www.mycloudbuddy.com/cbanalytics .html).

It's relatively easy to derive usage statistics for services such as S3 and CloudFront that directly deliver webpages to end users. Amazon S3 includes the ability to enable logging for a web-accessible bucket that produces log files in the same format as would a local server. These log files can be processed through any of the standard tools for generating usage reports from a web server, including free utilities such as Webalizer (http://www.webalizer.com/) and AWStats (http://awstats.sourceforge.net/) as well as more sophisticated commercial analytics tools such as WebTrends (http://www.webtrends.com/). As libraries make use of many different applications within the web environment, they need to regularly download and process the log files to generate usage reports.

Libraries can also implement tools such as Google Analytics that use a technique called "page tagging" as the basis for reports and analysis of all the components of the web presence. Page tagging involves inserting a small snippet of JavaScript that transmits relevant data elements for each page request to be recorded on the servers of the analytics engine. Google Analytics is free and provides detailed and sophisticated reports that a library can use to monitor usage patterns and discern trends for each of its web-based services. Each of the web-based applications used by an organization within its domain can be registered and tracked separately. Tracking is enabled by inserting the JavaScript provided in the Google Analytics registration process into the header of each page delivered. For static websites, this code can be placed in a file common to each page. Most dynamically generated sites include procedures that allow the insertion of custom elements such as the Google Analytics tracking code. Each site registered through the library's Google Analytics account will be assigned a unique tracking code. In the library context, this approach makes it easy to monitor the relative use and interest in each of the major components of its environment, such as the general website, the online catalog to the ILS, discovery interfaces, and various digital collections.

Google Analytics provides a wealth of information regarding the use of a website, including the standard metrics like page views, sessions, unique visitors, and bounce rate. Based on the referrer data, it presents information on the pathways that users followed to reach your site. For the visits that come through search engines, it is able to track the specific keywords that users entered. This referral data is especially important as it helps tune and optimize the site relative to its performance in search engines, which we noted in Chapter 6 as an important aspect of website marketing and promotion.

Cloud-based applications implemented by the library for use by patrons lend themselves to the page-tagging style of use monitoring as embraced by Google Analytics. Given that applications deployed through the various cloud-based deployment models may have different internal methods for measuring and analyzing use, Google Analytics provides a consistent view of all applications that comprise the library's web presence. It easily monitors website usage, observing its initial uptake and its growth over time. It helps assess whether library users easily find a new service or if they appear to have difficulties in using it. Finally, Google Analytics takes an action-oriented approach, supporting the practice of making iterative changes and demonstrating whether they have a positive or negative impact on the use of the resource.

▶ ASSESS STRATEGIC IMPACT

While many tools measure the levels of use of any given service, it is more challenging to measure how well the services accomplish their intended functions or if they make a positive contribution to the strategic activities of the library. As part of the general assessment of any given project, product, or service, one of the key tasks includes creating data that demonstrate its impact on the library's broader goals and not just measure how much churn of activity it produces.

Libraries can use an assessment survey such as LibQUAL+ (http://libqual .org/home) to measure whether its information and technology tools provide a positive user experience. While the questions offered by a general survey may not necessarily hone in on very specific components of the library's technology environment, it is possible to measure the broad impact by analyzing survey results over a multiyear period. LibQUAL+, for example, includes a section on Information Control, including questions about remote access to electronic resources, the library's website, and availability of electronic information. It, or others that a library might license or construct for itself, can help assess the performance of the overall infrastructure supporting access of information and services to patrons. By analyzing the results of an assessment instrument deployed over an extended period of time, the library can help shed light on the performance of specific services. Such a process might answer such questions as whether the implementation of a major new patron-facing platform such as a new discovery system or a revamped library website results in an increase or decrease in patron satisfaction in the year following the implementation relative to the previous year.

Much of the technology a library implements relates to the delivery of content to users. The performance of these products and projects should be reflected in the use patterns of the resources to which they provide access. The main premise of discovery services lies in the need to provide patrons with better tools to find and gain access to all the different kinds of content that comprise the library's collections. The online catalogs of ILSs provide access primarily to books and other physical objects, while the library's article collections, offered through subscriptions to electronic resources, are accessed through various types of finding aids, with some available through federated search tools. Discovery systems aim to provide a more efficient and user-friendly approach to searching all library resources through a single search box. It should be possible to measure their success by comparing detailed usage patterns of these resources prior to implementation with those after the implementation. To measure the impact of a new discovery service or other major interface that alters the way that patrons gain access to library collections, it's essential to have detailed statistics on the use of each collection component collected over time. These usage patterns can then be correlated with the deployment timetable of the new services to demonstrate their impact.

These are just some ideas regarding ways to measure the performance and impact of some of the cloud-based services implemented by a library. As seen throughout this book, cloud computing covers a very wide range of possible applications in a library context. Each category of use will come with its own possibilities for gathering usage data. Some applications used more informally may not require as much attention in this area, whereas strategic applications that play a direct role in the operation of some part of the library or in the delivery of its services to users demand more rigorous assessment. Some of the general principles that might apply across all types of cloud computing deployed might include activating and exploiting any opportunity to collect use data, such as any optional logging features, capturing any available data related to the operational context of the application, and continually monitoring any dashboards or statistical reports that reveal patterns of use. As with any new technology, its value needs to be supported as strongly as possible through empirical data rather than through more informal means such as a rationale that it is in line with current tech trends or is "cool." All technology projects that involve significant library resources may be subject to justification, and collecting and analyzing some of the metrics will be essential to make a business case in their support.

▶9

DEVELOPING TRENDS

- ▶ **Expect a Shift in Library IT Personnel and Budgets**
- ▶ **Look for New Products Built on the Cloud**
- ▶ **Know That Traditional Architectures Will Persist**
- ▶ **Expect a Movement toward Web-Based Interfaces and Lightweight Apps**
- ▶ **Recognize the Constraints of Connectivity**
- ▶ **Watch Companies Push the Limits**

There's no unringing the bell of cloud computing. This model of computing has become well established in the mainstream of information technology, and we can anticipate that it will become increasingly dominant over time. Other than this broad generality, there are some other trends that will likely play out over time to which libraries should pay attention as they think about their future technology plans. This chapter makes some general observations on some of the trends related to cloud computing playing out today and some projections where this technology might be heading in the future.

▶EXPECT A SHIFT IN LIBRARY IT PERSONNEL AND BUDGETS

Earlier chapters have described how cloud computing displaces local equipment with a major impact on the technology support personnel. As a result of increased deployments of cloud-based services, we can expect libraries to shift their technology personnel to be less involved in support of low-level maintenance of equipment and network infrastructure. Libraries may need fewer IT personnel overall, or they may reorient these individuals to take on new projects that use their talents to create new kinds of services. The technology trend of cloud computing brings some impact to long-term personnel planning for libraries.

In other cases, realities of personnel may help drive the trend toward cloud computing. Many libraries do not have adequate in-house technology personnel and therefore may gravitate toward automation infrastructure based on cloud services accordingly. It seems that both the technology trends and the personnel trends complement each other, pulling the libraries increasingly toward reliance on software applications deployed through one of the varieties of cloud computing.

► LOOK FOR NEW PRODUCTS BUILT ON THE CLOUD

Most new technology products and services will be created and deployed through some flavor of cloud computing. Software developers and consumers alike see great advantage in web-based services that don't require all the headaches involved with maintaining servers and desktop clients. Building new applications from scratch affords the opportunity to make use of current-day technologies and architectures, which in this era would involve such things as service-oriented architecture implemented through cloud-based platforms. A scan of some of the recently developed or announced library-specific products confirms this trend. OCLC's WorldShare Management Services, Ex Libris's Alma, Serials Solutions' Intota, Springshare's LibGuides, BiblioCommons, and DuraCloud are (or will be) delivered through SaaS.

► KNOW THAT TRADITIONAL ARCHITECTURES WILL PERSIST

Yet, traditional, locally installed software will be with us for a very long time. It's an established model of computing that is well suited for many scenarios. Very complex business applications for large organizations, for example, continue to defy what might be reasonably accommodated in a multitenant SaaS deployment. Large organizations with enterprise networks laden with complex, interrelated business applications may move toward building out their own private cloud infrastructure to gain some of the efficiencies of a highly consolidated and virtualized computing environment.

In the realm of library-specific software, we can expect established products to evolve to adopt more of the characteristics of cloud technologies even as new products launch inherently designed to be deployed as a service. We already see a number of ILSs originally designed for installation on servers local to the library and accessed by graphical desktop clients taking at least small steps in the direction of cloud computing. Almost all of the traditional ILS products have been tamed to operate in a virtualized server environment, with a strong trend toward vendor-hosting arrangements following an SaaS business model. Over time web-based applications are displacing desktop graphical clients for these established products, usually on a module-by-module basis. Whether through an evolutionary process or through displacement by next-generation products, we can expect the library automation landscape ten years from now to be dominated by SaaS and other cloud technologies.

▶ EXPECT A MOVEMENT TOWARD WEB-BASED INTERFACES AND LIGHTWEIGHT APPS

On the desktop, web-based interfaces will increasingly prevail, with optional apps for advanced users. An important component of a cloud-friendly design involves eliminating the need for workstation clients that are installed, configured, and periodically updated. The thick desktop applications that emerged in an era dominated by client/server computing seem unwieldy in today's milieu of cloud computing that favors pure web-based interfaces or lightweight apps. Most modern cloud services such as Google Apps completely avoid installable desktop software. But this tendency isn't universal. Consider services such as Twitter delivered natively through a web interface, though most devoted users make use of one of the many client apps, such as TweetDeck. Mobile users especially gravitate toward apps that can deliver a more sophisticated and usable interface than pure mobile web access.

Delivering all functionality through a web-based interface and applications helps to achieve the kind of computing efficiencies associated with cloud computing. In the library context, the complexities involved in presenting an interface that deals with all types of data entry techniques and other routine tasks such as editing MARC records while maintaining the level of keyboarding efficiencies essential for high-productivity environments isn't easy to accomplish with the basic controls available in HTML-based webforms. Fortunately, over the years web-based interfaces have become much more sophisticated, narrowing their limitations relative to full-blown graphical clients. We can expect almost all new applications to deliver a fully functional web interface.

The movement to all-web-based clients for library personnel to operate the functions of library automation systems has been slow and gradual. We see some cases where a web-based version of a module with a simplified subset of functionality is available for situations that do not demand the full functionality built into the graphical client. But most of the established ILSs demand a full-blown graphical client to operate their full feature set with reasonable efficiency. In the previous development cycle, we saw some library automation vendors develop or migrate their graphical clients into a Java environment, allowing them to operate on any computer that supported the Java Runtime Environment (JRE) rather than being confined to a single operating system such as Microsoft Windows or Macintosh. These Java applications can offer a rich graphical interface with all the nuanced controls of native application but with more portability. The overhead of the JRE unfortunately requires more computing resources, especially in terms of processor and memory demands, than native applications. The need to maintain beefy desktop computers to run the client applications and to deal with refreshing these clients with every major upgrade of the system continues to rank as one of the most onerous tasks associated with the maintenance of many ILSs. The ongoing progression toward cloud computing promises to reduce this burden.

Front-end library interfaces intended for library patrons have embraced cloud computing technologies at a faster pace than the back-end automation systems used by library personnel. In Chapter 3 we noted that many of the new discovery services increasingly are based on cloud technologies such as multi-tenant SaaS and highly shared data services. Libraries have been much more successful at providing web-based applications for all the services directed toward library patrons. Web-based online catalogs rapidly replaced graphical modules long ago. Unfortunately the development of these web-based online catalogs stagnated as other consumer-oriented applications advanced rapidly, delivering modern streamlined interfaces. Only in recent years have next-generation library catalogs or discovery services revitalized these interfaces to operate on a par with the expectations of library users relative to the other destinations they experience on the web.

▶ RECOGNIZE THE CONSTRAINTS OF CONNECTIVITY

Full ubiquity of cloud computing will be constrained by the limitations in connectivity to the Internet. The viability of cloud computing depends on fast and reliable bandwidth essential for users to access applications and data that reside remotely in some cloud infrastructure.

Unfortunately, we seem to be pretty far away from the point of universal connectivity. Many rural and remote areas continue to lack adequate bandwidth. Even areas where connectivity generally is more abundant, it's not possible to be online all the time. In the course of a day, one can move among wired connections, WiFi, and cellular data service and still not be connected all the time. In the current state of intermittent service opportunities, it can be a challenge to maintain productivity when totally dependent on connectivity to the cloud.

Some of the current trends placing caps on data use also run counter to the demands of cloud computing services. In recent months cellular data providers and home broadband services have begun to move away from unlimited data transmission, imposing additional fees when use exceeds designated thresholds. Video and other multimedia content have an enormous appetite for bandwidth, causing some network operators to impose limits to help ensure that the capacity of their infrastructure meets demand. The availability and cost of bandwidth is a concern although in itself is not likely to impede the trend toward increased adoption of cloud computing.

▷ WATCH COMPANIES PUSH THE LIMITS

A number of companies will push cloud computing to its fullest extent. Google, for example, continues to develop products that support an aggressive cloud strategy. All of its products embrace the cloud computing concepts we've covered throughout this book to the extreme. Google Apps, the Google App Engine, all its Search products, Google Maps, Google Earth, Google Analytics, YouTube, Google Blogs (formerly Blogger), and its dozens of other products and services epitomize the vision of cloud computing. Given its laser focus on cloud computing, Google also develops a lot of supporting infrastructure. It developed the Chrome web browser, for example, to deliver the fastest and easiest experience of the web possible. By July 2011, Google's Chrome browser represented over 20 percent of all web traffic, with use of Microsoft's Internet Explorer dropping quickly and Mozilla Firefox dipping slightly.

Taking the concept of cloud computing to its logical limit, Google also developed the Chrome operating system, designed with the sole purpose of connecting users to applications in the cloud. The Chrome OS does not include support for running typical desktop applications but rather uses the Chrome web browser as its sole user interface. A laptop computer running the Chrome OS will boot in a few seconds to the Chrome web browser ready to connect to the web. Google partnered with manufacturers, currently Acer and Samsung, to create the "Chromebook," an inexpensive laptop computer specifically built to run the Chrome OS and the Chrome web browser with connectivity through WiFi or 3G cellular data service. Chromebooks only run applications that can be delivered through a web browser or apps written specifically for the Chrome web browser, of which there are thousands. These devices do not run applications designed for operating systems like Windows or Macintosh. Chromebooks do not include disk drives or other local storage devices, because all the applications will store their data within their cloud environment.

The key limitation of the approach embraced by Chromebooks lies in their uselessness when they can't connect to the Internet. Few of the cloud-based applications, including Google's own apps, include an offline mode where users can continue to work when not connected. These devices tie productivity directly to connectivity, which in the real world is riddled with interruptions. Early reviews of the Chromebooks have not been especially positive, mostly citing the uselessness of the device when not connected and the expense of needing to be connected to perform any kind of work.

The Chromebook may be a bit ahead of its time. Most of the world just doesn't have the kind of connectivity needed to support its thorough reliance on the cloud nor do the apps have the capability to operate offline. But it does seem like we're heading down that path. While today's tech environment is beginning to reorient itself more toward cloud-based technologies in both the consumer and business worlds, it's at a middle stage of transition where a few substantial obstacles remain. It also seems that these obstacles may be eroding and that it would be feasible to expect cloud computing to grow into an even more dominant position within a relatively short period.

RECOMMENDED READING

Anderson, Janna, and Lee Rainie. 2011. *The Future of Cloud Computing*. Pew Internet & American Life Project. June 11. http://pewinternet.org/Reports/2010/The-future-of-cloud-computing.aspx.

> Pew Internet gathers data and provides excellent analysis on a variety of topics relevant to libraries. How the general public makes use of different technologies provides an important context to the way that libraries deliver their services. This study on the future of cloud computing provides a useful gauge on the forward trends that cloud computing is expected to gain in future years.

Beil, Joshua, Bob Egan, Mark Fidelman, Jeffrey Kaplan, Karl Scott, and Joe Tierney. 2010. *2011 Trends Report: Cloud Computing*. Focus Research. December 30. http://media.focus.com/assets/research-briefing/2011-trends-report-cloud-computing/TR-cloud-computing-2.pdf.

> This industry report, authored by a panel of experts in the field, provides analysis at the broader information technology sector regarding the inevitable increased adoption of cloud computing and its impact on business. The report also includes insights into the impact of cloud technologies on mobile computing.

Breeding, Marshall. 2009. "In Challenge to ILS Industry, OCLC Extends WorldCat Local to Launch New Library System." *Library Journal*. April 23. http://www.libraryjournal.com/article/CA6653619.html.

> OCLC's WorldShare Management Services represents an approach to library automation most closely associated with cloud technologies. This article describes OCLC's vision for the product, some of its expected features, and the expected time frame for deployment.

———. 2009. "Systems Librarian Column: The Advance of Computing from the Ground to the Cloud." *Computers in Libraries* 29, no. 10 (Nov./Dec.): 22–26. http://www.librarytechnology.org/ltg-displaytext.pl?RC=14384.

> This column provides a very general overview of cloud computing and how it is being adopted by some of the major companies involved in library automation. The essay describes a progress of technologies evolving from locally housed computing through increasing levels of abstraction to more pure cloud computing models.

———. 2011. "Library Discovery: From the Ground to the Cloud." In *Getting Started with Cloud Computing: A LITA Guide,* edited by Edward M. Corrado and Heather Lea Moulaison, 71–86. New York: Neal-Schuman.

This chapter focuses on library resource discovery products and how they have increasingly taken on characteristics of cloud technologies. This genre of software has evolved from ones locally installed that provide modern interfaces for accessing library collections to ones based on large indexes maintained in a cloud environment that provide more comprehensive access, including massive aggregations of scholarly e-journal content at the article level.

Buck, Stephanie. 2009. "Libraries in the Cloud: Making a Case for Google and Amazon." *Computers in Libraries* 29, no. 8 (Sep.): 6–10.

This feature begins with a general explanatory discussion of cloud computing, its impact on the general IT industry, and how it is the basis of the technical platforms of the major organizations such as Google and Amazon.com. This technology has major implications for libraries, as cited in the way that Boston Public Library has made use of cloud services such as S3 from Amazon Web Services.

Cervone, H. Frank. 2010. "Managing Digital Libraries at 30,000 Feet: An Overview of Virtual and Cloud Computing." *OCLC Systems and Services: International Digital Library Perspectives* 26, no. 3: 162–165.

Cervone provides a technical, but accessible, explanation of the technologies surrounding cloud computing and its various flavors.

Corrado, Edward M., and Heather Lea Moulaison, eds. 2011. *Getting Started with Cloud Computing: A LITA Guide.* New York: Neal-Schuman.

This book contains chapters written by a variety of authors, each of whom brings different experiences and applications to cloud computing, primarily in a library setting.

Goodman, Amanda. 2011. "Cloud Computing in Libraries and Library School." AmandaGoodman.com. Accessed June 15. http://www.amandagoodman.com/cloud-computing-in-libraries-and-library-school/.

This essay, written from the perspective of a graduate student in a library and information science program, provides a general introduction to cloud computing and suggests ways that these technologies can be adopted within a graduate department's office.

Gorman, Zoe. "Yale E-mail to Move to Google." *Yale Daily News,* April 18. http://www.yaledailynews.com/news/2011/apr/18/yale-email-to-move-to-google/.

This article provides an example of the general trend for colleges and universities to move away from locally operated commodity services, such as e-mail, to an outsourced arrangement based on software-as-a-service.

Guess, Andy. 2007. "When E-mail Is Outsourced." *Inside Higher Ed.* November 27. http://www.insidehighered.com/news/2007/11/27/email.

Written in 2007, this article shows, even at that early date relative to the broad acceptance of cloud computing, some of the practical advantages for colleges and universities to consider outsourcing resource-intensive services such as e-mail for students to external providers.

Jones, Don. 2010. *Strategies for Cloud Storage, Data Protection, and Disaster Recovery.* White Paper, sponsored by i365, a Seagate Company, in The Essentials Series, published by Realtime Publishers. http://pages.i365.com/rs/i365/images Strategies%20for%20 Cloud%20Storage,%20Data%20Protection,%20and%20 Disaster%20Recovery.pdf.

This technical white paper, written from the perspective of a company with business interests in cloud computing, describes some of the concerns with mounting critical data only on cloud storage and some strategies to consider to ensure data integrity and disaster recovery capabilities.

Katz, Richard N., ed. 2008. *The Tower and the Cloud: Higher Education in the Age of Cloud Computing.* EDUCAUSE E-book. http://www.educause.edu/thetowerandthecloud.

This freely available e-book contains chapters authored by a variety of experts on topics related to the use of information technology in higher education. While the general context lies in the premise that cloud technologies will be an increasing aspect of information in higher education, the essays generally involve higher-level topics.

Krill, Paul. "Cloud Computing: Threat or Opportunity." *InfoWorld* (blog), May 31. http://www.infoworld.com/t/cloud-computing/cloud-computing-threat-or-opportunity-624.

This essay focuses on the impact of cloud computing on organizations, especially on potential of the technology to allow reductions in the number of IT personnel. For IT personnel, increased reliance on cloud computing can represent a threat to their role within the organization.

Kroski, Ellyssa. 2009. "Library Cloud Atlas: A Guide to Cloud Computing and Storage." *Library Journal.* October 10. http://www.libraryjournal.com/article/CA6695772.html.

This article provides clear definitions for the various technologies associated with cloud computing and cites ways that specific libraries have incorporated it into their operations.

Mitchell, Erik. 2010. "Using Cloud Services for Library IT Infrastructure." *Code4lib Journal* 9, no. 2010-03-22. http://journal.code4lib.org/articles/2510.

The article describes the three categories of cloud computing—software-as-a-service, infrastructure-as-a-service, and platform-as-a-service. Following the technology overview, Mitchell describes how the Z. Smith Reynolds Library at Wake Forest University made use of each of these approaches.

Peters, Chris. 2010. "What Is Cloud Computing and How Will It Affect Libraries?" *TechSoup for Libraries* (blog), March 6. http://www.techsoupforlibraries.org/blog/ what-is-cloud-computing-and-how-will-it-affect-libraries.

Peters summarizes some of the benefits of cloud computing, such as cost savings and flexibility for innovation, as well as the changes and opportunities it brings to the organization's IT personnel. The article mentions the emerging options for implementing a cloud-based ILS or discovery service.

Pogue, David. 2011. "A Laptop, Its Head in the Cloud." *New York Times,* June 15. http://www.nytimes.com/2011/06/16/technology/personaltech/16pogue.html.

Pogue reviews the Chromebook, a laptop designed to run the Chrome operating system, delivering all functionality through the Chrome web browser, generally concluding that its pure cloud-based approach may not be practical for today's world of intermittent connectivity.

Ried, Stefan. 2011. "Sizing the Cloud." *Forrester Research* (blog), April 21. http://blogs.forrester.com/stefan_ried/11-04-21-sizing_the_cloud (summary given in a blog posting); http://forrester.com/rb/Research/sizing_cloud/q/id/58161/t/2 (website where report can be purchased).

Forrester performs systematic assessments of new technologies, projections of adoption, and risks and benefits. This survey of cloud computing is designed to help IT managers make decisions regarding adoption of the technology. The introduction to the report summarizes trends and projections; the full report is available only to Forrester subscribers and for purchase.

Wheeler, Brad, and Shelton Wagoner. 2011. "Above-Campus Services: Shaping the Promise of Cloud Computing for Higher Education." *EDUCAUSE Review* 44, no. 6 (May/June). http://www.educause.edu/EDUCAUSE+Review/EDUCAUSEReview MagazineVolume44/AboveCampusServicesShapingtheP/185222.

Authored by two leading information technology administrators in major universities, this article explores how cloud technologies enable new ways of supporting higher education through "above-campus" models sourcing services to commercial providers, institutions, and consortia.

INDEX

ABOUT THE AUTHOR

Marshall Breeding is an internationally known library technologist, writer, speaker, and consultant. He serves as the Director for Innovative Technologies and Research for the Vanderbilt University Library and as the Executive Director of the Vanderbilt Television News Archive. Breeding has previously edited or authored six books. His monthly column "Systems Librarian" appears in *Computers in Libraries*; he is the editor for *Smart Libraries Newsletter*, published by the American Library Association, and has authored the annual "Automation Marketplace" feature published by *Library Journal* since 2002. He has authored eight issues of ALA's *Library Technology Reports* and has written many other articles and book chapters. His most recent issue of *Library Technology Reports* was titled "Open Source Integrated Library Systems." He is on the editorial board of *The Electronic Library*, published by Emerald Group, and *Information Standards Quarterly*, published by NISO. He was the recipient of the 2010 LITA/Library Hi Tech Award for Outstanding Communication in Library and Information Technology. Breeding is the creator and editor of Library Technology Guides (www.librarytechnology.org) and the lib-web-cats online directory. He regularly teaches workshops and gives presentations at library conferences on a wide range of topics. He is a regular presenter at Computers in Libraries and Internet Librarian conferences, is a LITA Top Technology Trends panelist at ALA conferences, and has been an invited speaker for many library conferences and workshops throughout the United States and internationally. He has spoken throughout the United States and in Argentina, Colombia, Korea, Taiwan, Thailand, China, Singapore, the Czech Republic, Austria, Slovenia, the Netherlands, Norway, Sweden, Denmark, and the United Kingdom.

Facet Publishing is wholly owned by CILIP: the Chartered Institute of Library and Information Professionals.

First published in the USA by ALA TechSource, an imprint of the American Library Association, 2012.
This simultaneous UK edition 2012.

British Library Cataloguing in Publication Data
A catalogue record for this book is available from the British Library.

ISBN 978-1-85604-847-7

Printed and bound in the United Kingdom.

THE TECH SET

11

d
g
s

JG

IC
olitan Colleg
d LRC

facet publishing